Women in My Office

By Charles Herrick

Published by Human Fabric Publishing

Seattle, Washington

Women in My Office

Registered with the United States Copyright Office

ISBN: 1451579888

EAN-13: 9781451579888

Printed in the United States of America

Cover photo: The author's great-grandmother Rose

Other Books by Charles Herrick

Breath of Kenya, Medicine, Mystery and Women in Rural Kenya (Non-fiction)

Alone in a primitive village in Africa to help create an economy, the appearance of a silent, deadly epidemic leads to a new, somewhat dangerous role. Charles has to play village doctor treating life-threatening diseases that most in the West have never seen. Lots of interesting insights on African life, told with humor, mixed with drama. A greatly expanded version of the original book *Breath of Kenya*, this puts more focus on the strange rituals and taboos – especially those involving women. More little stories and some added drama.

A Checkerboard (Fiction, based on a real story)

A very white enlisted man rides through Mississippi on a bus of only black soldiers at the end of World War II. Simpson will prove the power of naiveté in changing the world around him. He settles in northern Mississippi where he courts a Southern Belle, partners with a black house painter and is taken under the wing of an aging matriarch. His cultural tutors are everywhere but led most prominently by an old black butler and a tough army Sergeant. Both support him through the cultural maze and intrigue of Southern living.

Purple Boy (Non-fiction, autobiography)

A fascinating, often light-hearted look at a pretty tough childhood, set against the backdrop of a special year running track. This in turn is woven into a psychological exploration of what is causing a sleep disorder developed in adulthood. Humor and drama bring forth the message that the human spirit can wade through anything.

A Guide to Managing Earthlings (Business management)

IBM-style management philosophy is mixed with the author's unique style to cover everything from personnel management to corporate strategy. *What* trumps *How;* and real managers take the place of jerk bosses in this hard-hitting guide, filled with humor, war stories and personal insights. It can serve as a baseline for *Women in My Office*.

Visit CharlesHerrick.com

To the many women in Africa, India and Romania

Who became my friends.

Though they will never have the opportunities

That women elsewhere in the world enjoy,

They are lovely and alive,

Ready to take on each day

With courage and character,

Which I will forever admire

But never fully comprehend.

TABLE OF CONTENTS

Preface

It was my favorite Jewish lady, an IBM friend, who made me realize all these conversations I was having with women in my office were neither random nor just part of an executive's job.

As I occasionally did, I joined her and three other IBM women for a cup of coffee a few blocks down the street from our Seattle office building. It had been an especially interesting conversation in that they would frequently forget there was a guy sitting with them.

At one point, they were talking about a Sylvester Stallone movie that had just come out called *Cliffhanger.* In the opening scene, a man and a woman made an arduous rock climb and were stuck on top of a needle-thin peak. So they had to be rescued by Sylvester Stallone who was delivered via Forest Service helicopter. They were on a rock 8000 feet in the air, about to rappel across an abyss, when Stallone asked this frail woman, a novice who had just made a massively difficult climb, how she had gotten talked into scaling The Tower? She responded, "He told me it was better than sex."

The women in my coffee klatch, all in their late thirties and early forties, laughed and agreed that a guy must have written that line. "There is no way I am going to climb more than two flights of stairs for something better than sex," one of them declared. "Tell him to send me a picture from up there. Okay, so I'm cut off. I think I'll be all right," my Jewish friend offered.

As we were leaving the table, she put her hand on my shoulder and said casually, "I was hoping my friend Sylvia could come by and talk to you later today. She recently went through a divorce and she just wants someone to listen to her, I think. I told her you had a good ear for her to bend."

"Boy, I never keep up on these things. People have affairs and die and get divorced then I hear about it a year later."

"She's not an IBMer. She's just a friend. She and her husband moved out here six months ago and then he left her. She really doesn't have anyone else to talk to. Can you spend some time with her?"

"The human side of me says, 'Yes, of course,' but normally I talk mostly to people in my organization and I..."

"That's not true. You talk to everybody. People are always coming to your office. Even people who don't like you talk to you about personal stuff."

"Who doesn't like me...?" (There were a few, trust me. I just wanted specifics).

"Anyway, I told Sylvia about 2 o'clock. I checked your calendar with your secretary. That works for you," she tossed out, dryly – kind of like, "Just do your job."

I asked my secretary Theresa if she saw things the way my friend did, regarding people talking to me. She said, "Yeah, pretty much." She then told me that when an attractive woman came to my office, she would often stay around, rather than go to break or lunch - "Because bad things can just suddenly happen, even with a loyal husband." It really never occurred to me. And I don't think it ever occurred to the women I was talking to. I believe they viewed me as safe. (I'm not entirely sure how to take that). However, Theresa was near retirement and she had seen enough in her time. She had been doing sentry duty for over two years and I never knew it.

One thing you have to possess is the ability to hold a confidence. For that reason, none of the names will be real in the situations in this book.

To show how seriously I take it when someone talks to me about a confidential issue, here's a humorous example from when I was a CEO at a Seattle high tech firm. My administrative assistant came into my office and said, "I have something to tell you but I don't want you to mention it to anyone. Okay?" I of course agreed. She stepped closer and whispered, "I just found out I'm pregnant." I congratulated her and we chatted for a bit. It was to be her first child.

A little over a month later, she showed up at my door, looking none too happy.

"What's up?" I asked, trying to interpret the somewhat stony countenance.

"I just talked to your wife. She said she didn't even *know* I'm pregnant."

"You told me not to tell anyone. So I didn't."

"Well that didn't mean Kristy!"

"You didn't say, 'Don't tell anyone except for Kristy.'"

Later I got a lecture from my wife.

So, my administrative assistant felt that I didn't care enough to tell Kristy; and Kristy thought I was keeping important information from her. I was 0 for 2, with no more times at bat.

The truth is I hate it when I ask someone to hold onto a piece of information I am giving them and then they start making a list of the people they want to tell - "if it's okay." So I don't do that. Once people question your willingness to keep a confidence, they will quit telling you things. Being naturally curious, I usually am very interested to learn about the things that affect the lives of my fellow earthlings.

* * *

The subject of generalizing about women needs to be addressed in advance.

I noticed an odd thing when I discussed my concern about generalizing and stereotyping. Women had a lot less trouble with it than men. It could just be politically correct over-sensitivity on the part of men these days. Or it could be that women know they have common issues which are unique to women. Besides, they were really curious to read what I had to say. For those reasons, women were the most encouraging for me to write this book. A couple of them had previously spent hours with me on the phone discussing issues of their own. They knew the value of just having someone they could talk to.

I had two big concerns when starting to write which were hard to get around. First, I didn't want to come across as condescending - like I had all the answers. I don't even pretend to. What I'm trying to do in this book is lay out some important and interesting situations and some of the intriguing problems these women faced. It would not make sense to present a series of inconclusive discussions. I would get frustrated just writing about them and I know the reader wouldn't like it. These are the stories where I actually *did* have an answer, right or wrong.

Second, and most important, I didn't want to paint a picture portraying all women as the same; as if the two X chromosomes are somehow wrapped around a woman's ankles and she'll fall flat if she tries to move away from her gender's stereotypes. Women have an incredible range and diversity of thought and as many different approaches to life as there are women. I know that. But anyone who would say the two genders are nearly identical is bending reality for some odd reason.

* * *

The women who came to see me weren't thinking about any of this stuff. They were just trying to find a way back to level ground. And they needed someone they could talk to.

It was a mixture of hope and trust and sometimes sheer desperation that caused one woman after another over a period of 15 years to sit across the desk from me, draw a deep breath, and begin to tell me her story.

Women in My Office

Cynthia

Betrayal is often thought of in terms of a specific act. But it's not. The act of betrayal is in reality the outward manifestation of devaluing another human being to the point where you are willing to hurt them. All betrayal causes hurt. But not every hurt, including one that creates a lot of damage, is necessarily the product of a willful betrayal.

Cynthia was hurt. But was she betrayed?

That morning I got to work early, before 7 AM, in order to catch up on a bunch of things that were due shortly. The only other car in the parking garage that day was a familiar, blue VW Beetle with a Garfield cat suction-cupped to one of the rear windows. I thought how irritating it would be to have to stare at that every time you changed lanes. But I also thought it was kind of nice that someone was willing to put up with a bigger blind spot so we could all stare at something silly during our commute. I soon found out whose car it was.

When I got to my office I saw Cynthia sitting at Sharon's desk, instead of her own desk which was around the corner. She had a direct view of my office door that way. As I unlocked my door, I wondered how long she had been sitting there. Having someone waiting to see me an hour or more before work had happened previously, but never with Cynthia.

Then she asked the question which was built around the greatest misestimate of time in Newtonian physics, "Do you have a minute?"

"Good morning, Cynthia. How long have you been here?"

"A long time."

I talked her into letting me make some coffee. One of the first things I do when I take over as manager of a new location is upgrade the coffee and brewing equipment. We had gourmet Arabica coffees from around the world and 208 Volt commercial brewers — right next to the behemoth espresso machine. We chatted about coffee and other banalities because we both knew the kitchen was not the place for her to share what was on her mind.

When we were in my office, I offered her a seat. I did not turn on my computer; I did not check for messages even though the red message light was on. When someone comes to talk to you they want your full attention. People who check their computer and their text messages, while saying "Uh huh," to let you know they're still listening are a blight on civilization. You instantly devalue another person by doing that.

This was one morning Cynthia needed anything but that.

"I'm not sure I'm going to be any good at work the rest of the week," she started, without looking up.

"If you need some personal time off, Cynthia, don't worry about it. Do you want to talk about it?" Remember, it was 6:50 in the morning. Of course she wanted to talk about it.

"You don't really want to hear about my screwed up life and stupid problems."

My cue.

"I always want to hear about an issue someone's dealing with, if there's a possibility I can be of help. So what's going on?"

"I think I'm pregnant."

Relieved, I congratulated her. "So is that why you need some time off? If ever there was a good reason to take a break, it would be..."

"And my husband has been cheating on me."

I took off the party hat. "How do you know? — I mean, what makes you think so?"

"Because the doctor says the infection that I have I could only have gotten one of two ways. And I know which way I didn't pick it up."

"Is this a surprise?"

"Yes."

"Is it a complete surprise?"

"Yes."

I slumped in my chair and looked at her carefully. "Is it an unimaginable surprise — not the infection, but the stepping out?" This caused her to pause and reflect.

But her answer was the same. She did not and, in her opinion, could not see this coming. There was no sign. There had been no change in his behavior nor had there been any change in the way the two had been interacting.

The first notice she had received about her husband's behavior was a week ago, when the doctor told her that she had an infection. Her symptoms had been so mild that she almost didn't go. The doctor had seen a lot of this as sexual mores in society had become almost nonexistent. He delivered the news and treatment options as if it were a case of athlete's foot. He wasn't prepared for the etiological grilling and Cynthia's subsequent shocked response.

The next morning she woke up sick to her stomach. After three days of nausea, she realized that it wasn't grief. She thought she might be pregnant. Being a month and three days off in her cycle, she knew her appointment this afternoon would confirm that she was a mother-to-be. She could have bought an over-the-counter pregnancy test but she didn't want to take it, wonder if it was correct and then go see a doctor anyway - just as all her friends had done.

Cynthia was 28. What a way to start a family.

I thought back on each of our three pregnancies and what joyous moments they were. Even knowing the tough road ahead which would involve a C-section, Kristy couldn't wait to get on the phone and tell people. Her only low moments were when she would say, "I wish my mom was still alive." As I mentioned earlier, Kristy's mom, from whom she had inherited her delicate features and so much of her sweetness, had died when Kristy was 16. On the few times Kristy had that reflection, I admired her strength. She always seemed to move on, even though her mom had been her best friend.

This was not the first time a woman I knew had been cheated on. It was also not the first time the woman held herself to be significantly to blame. Cynthia sounded like she held herself about 80% to blame.

There were a lot of words. I listened as she went back and forth in her explanation for what had taken place. But the whole monologue netted out to this: "I've been working horrendous hours for over a year now. That's gotta be driving him nuts. And I come home looking haggard as hell. Some treat, huh?"

"So then, long hours and unbrushed hair cause infidelity?" I wanted to avoid using harsher terms than infidelity, which it was, because more than half the time, the wife ends up staying with her unfaithful husband, trying to make a go of it. Women often do this because they feel it will be difficult to find another man, especially when they are likely feeling even more worthless than normal. But beyond this, women are naturally far more monogamous than men. They innately believe the two have become one flesh and they don't wish to split that in half. It causes deep, deep injury. It's almost sad when women want to be married so much they will put up with a husband they have lost almost all affection for. If they have love for him in such an arrangement, it's a very left-handed love.

At first, they want to punish an unfaithful man by kicking him out of the house but they don't want to be unmarried. There was physiological civil war taking place on the other side of my desk. I was on her side but what does that mean? Does it mean I'm on her side and against her husband? Does that mean I'm on her side but against her marriage? Is that in her best interest? Is that really being on her side? I had to watch my step. There were landmines everywhere.

"Never being home and never looking nice doesn't help any," she said, weakly. She knew I wasn't going to buy it. The difficulty is she still probably thought she had contributed materially to the problem. If it wasn't long hours at the office and lack of physical attractiveness, she would find something else. This is the first phase. As often happens, she would soon be heading entirely in the opposite direction. She was unknowingly putting herself in the seat of a slingshot and steadily backing up.

When a guy is just a jerk and then he cheats, it's real simple. He cheated because he's a jerk. But when a "good" husband, a solid, loving guy cheats, a woman feels there has to be some exogenous driver. In her opinion, jerk or no jerk, she wasn't "woman enough" to keep her man. Personally and individually, this is what the woman believes. Collectively, women don't buy it when they see it happening to someone else.

I often hear shock and outrage when an athlete, screen celebrity, or politician cheats on his gorgeous wife. "But she was so beautiful! How could he? And did you see the woman he was having the affair with? She was nowhere near as pretty as his own wife."

When you are all alone and it's you, not some movie star's wife, then the needle points back at you. You assume the other woman is probably a little better looking, probably a bit younger, firmer and more fun. You immediately regret being such a prune at times. You regret going to the grocery store that Saturday without wearing makeup. You shouldn't be discussing your aches and pains and digestive issues. "I'm sure that's a turnoff!" you think.

I've heard it all.

Usually I just lean my head on my hand and look a bit incredulous without being disrespectful. I try to communicate subtly, "Do you really believe that?" or "Are you listening to yourself?" and "Does this sound as unrealistically nutty to you as it does to me?"

Here's a fact: almost all men want variety. Variety is spelled o-t-h-e-r-w-o-m-e-n. If this weren't true, then Playboy would have only needed to print one edition. However, some men let their wants lead them to actually doing something about those desires.

Life in society is about curbing most of our urges. We don't just take things we really want (or even desperately need) if they don't belong to us. We can't just punch people we are furious with, or shoot people who are ruining our lives. Society looks down on stealing, assault, and murder. But there's an odd morality message these days. In the movies and on TV, sex is a very casual thing. Sex on the first date is standard fare. The woman simply handles it like she just went to a good movie.

For a solid core of us, including most men I know, cheating on your wife is a rotten thing to do. It shows utterly low character – or at least a lapse. These days, it can even be deadly. When I was in college, there were three STDs, syphilis, gonorrhea, and herpes. Now there are 30 or more and some of them can kill you or render a woman sterile. Therefore, you curb those male instincts and you keep your original vows and commitments. Period.

But to a man who has sought to rationalize it, he now has plenty of examples in the public arena of "great" human beings who cheat on their wives and girlfriends – no real damage being done. The rationalization continues. "It's not like I don't still love my wife…" "This is just a short term deal. I'll tire of it and then everything will be back to normal…" "In the old days, men had lots of wives. It's natural. Look at the Old Testament. Solomon had about a thousand wives and he was a godly man." If you want to rationalize it, you can. It's still wrong. The guy knows it, but he feels he has at least lowered the moral threshold so that it isn't so obvious to himself that he's a blatant libertine.

All that being said about our adultery-nurturing culture, it's still his fault. Even if the woman has gained four hundred pounds and never combs her hair or bathes, he must keep his commitments. It is not her fault that he cheats and it's not society's fault that he cheats. It's not because his dad cheated. It's not because of all the semi-nude women who leer at us from the magazine covers in the checkout line at the grocery store. And it's not because he just got caught in the moment. He cheated because he chose to cheat.

Whether you believe in "sin" or not, you have a moral code of some kind. So, let me use the term "sin" for any violation of your accepted moral code, Biblical or otherwise, when I make this pronouncement about all the pressures on us to do wrong:

Here's a fact:

All sin is an inside job.

The devil didn't make you do it. You did it.

And if you're a woman, you didn't make him do it, he did it.

Cynthia was very attractive. But like all pretty women (no overbroad generalization here; the word is *all*) she can find enough wrong with herself that she knows she is not quite truly pretty. It's like some Greek myth, extended through the centuries, where someone is given a precious gift but they can never quite reach it or enjoy it.

I would say she looked like a runway model except for the fact that runway models these days look so weird to me that I would be doing a disservice to Cynthia in the comparison. Of course, it would have been inappropriate for me to tell her that. You can tell another woman her dress looks nice but that's where the pavement ends on the compliment road these days.

I listened to Cynthia for half an hour before starting to tell her about everything I've just written above. She had a lot to absorb. The best I could do was tell her over and over that it wasn't her fault; and then tell her over and over, that she would figure a way through all this.

People were just starting to come to work. A few momentarily stopped by my office and then decided not to interrupt. Cynthia sensed it was time to leave - for now. So she asked one last question, "What should I do tonight - I mean after Tom comes home? How do I act?"

"That's a big one, Cynthia. We need more time. Have you forgotten you have a very important doctor's appointment this afternoon?"

When I said that, she put her hand to her mouth and made a little gasp. She had momentarily forgotten something that could really complicate things. It could easily go from being an issue to being a mess and she knew it. Her eyes began to well up. She looked, and I'm sure she felt, utterly lost.

Since I had another office across the street, guarded by my faithful secretary Theresa, I asked her if she wanted to meet for a little while longer. The relief that spread over her face and the way she exhaled and let herself slump just a little answered the question. I picked up the phone to get Cynthia on my calendar and I only had to repeat it once when Theresa told me I had a conflict. She knew something was going on.

Cynthia showed up at exactly one o'clock. I couldn't tell if she was calmer or just exhausted. Prior to leaving our earlier meeting, I had suggested that she might want to see her most trusted clergyman. She didn't have one. How about mom or dad? Both dead.

"Do you have anyone else you trust?" I asked, trying to broaden her foundation of support.

9

"I don't want to spread this around at this point. If I talk to a bunch of people then they will be checking in on me endlessly. Everyone will want to know how I'm doing and I'll have to repeat my story and my status over and over. I just...I would feel better just keeping it a very small circle. Besides, I really don't know what I want my other friends to know at this point. I was hoping I could talk to you about that as well."

"You can talk to me about anything you want, Cynthia."

She had gone from being a lighthearted, near socialite, to a woman who was just barely hanging on. What a shame. Everyone enjoyed having her around. At 5 foot 11 and slender, with that unusual combination of red hair and brown eyes, she was possibly the most attractive woman in the building; yet she was just one of the gang. She did imitations of everyone, including me, but they were never mean-spirited. She was always up for lunch or an impromptu celebration. She often remembered other people's birthdays.

Now here she sat with that sense we all get at such times that your whole life up to this point has had little meaning because it has only led to this.

"I think tonight's going to be a mess. I almost don't want to go home. It's just going to be...it's going to be a terrible mess," she lamented, mostly to herself.

"I don't think so," I countered.

She looked surprised. "You don't? How could it not be?"

"It's only going to be a mess if you try to solve all the world's problems in one evening. I don't think you're ready to tackle the one issue and you don't know conclusively on the other topic — that of becoming a mom."

"So you are saying don't talk about him having an affair?"

"What's your final verdict and sentencing on that one?"

"In what way?" she asked, confused.

"In any way."

"I don't know."

"Then I'm saying it's not time to talk to him about having an affair. You're not ready. And this is one you really want to be ready for." I let it her absorb this. "You have one of two topics to deal with tonight: Either you're going to have a baby or you had a pregnancy test because you thought you were pregnant but you're not. Either of them would be a very rich source of conversation, but I would limit how much is said and then go to bed. You need sleep more than you need a discussion that you can only put half your heart into."

"I'll find it very hard to look at him," she said, defiantly, but veering more toward pitifully.

"I don't think that's true at all. I think you'll be looking at every move he makes, every smile, every tilt of his head. You'll listen for any hesitation in his voice, any platitudes or any sign of false excitement. Cynthia, you will be a one-woman radar station. Believe me."

"I suppose you're right."

"And that won't be good. Tonight is not a night to over-analyze. You are not in the best frame of mind and your filters are going to be malfunctioning. I would just keep it light and talk basics. If he's happy, just be pleasant."

"That makes sense."

"So, what if you're pregnant - what are you going to say?"

"I...I really don't know what I would want to say to him."

11

"Okay, then. Let's build you a foundation so you don't have to memorize a script. Let's start with how you feel about the idea of becoming a mom. How have you felt about that most of your life? What do you think of babies and kids in general? How many kids were you hoping to have? Do you want to know ahead of time which sex the baby is? I'm sure you've thought about these things at one time or another."

"Charles, I absolutely love kids," she said with some spirit. "I do. I've always wanted to be a mom. My mom was such a great mom and I want to be like her – like she was," her voice trailed off as she realized her mom wasn't here for this. Then she bounced back. "I want lots of kids. That's why I've been in such a hurry to get a family started. I actually wanted to get going a year ago but I had been…"

She stopped mid-sentence. I've never seen anyone burst into tears so suddenly and strongly. It was like being at the beach on a cloudless day and all of a sudden a thunderstorm opens up. It was loud enough that Theresa hovered outside the long vertical windows next to my doors. The windows had gauzy curtains and I could communicate by holding up my hand that it was okay – even though it didn't feel that way. Cynthia was in such pain. Empathetically, I had to fight back the tears myself. As I have already said, intimacy and commitment are such huge issues for a woman that men who cheat rarely have any idea of the damage they do. I knew. I was watching it. It was awful.

As painful as it was, she so needed this. Her spirit was completely constricted. I stood back and watched it fight for air and then breathe for the first time that day, or that week, for all I knew. The sobbing went on for what seemed like ten minutes but was probably five. Theresa had wisely put a new box of Kleenex on my desk. I don't know how she knew to do that.

People who cry seem to get really thirsty. I offered to get her some water but she declined. I asked Theresa to get her some anyway. She needed water in her system for everything she was going to go through that day.

Women often say they're sorry when they finish crying. But I don't think it's an apology as much as it's just some type of punctuation. Crying, to some women, is an extended figure of speech. It needs something on the end of it in order to move to the next paragraph in the conversation.

"Cynthia, you really need one of your friends to..."

"I don't have anyone that I'm that close to. Tom was my best friend and I kind of cut other people out of my life. I've always felt a bit bad about that but not really. It just...it was so nice. We had..."

Once again the tears flowed. That was my last attempt to get her to share with others what she was discussing with me. This made it really hard because I just couldn't stay in this role for a prolonged period of time – certainly not to this level of involvement. But if I told her that before tonight, she would feel incredibly alone. If I waited until the next day, she would feel like she had overburdened me and leaned on the wrong person.

Oy.

"What if he's all excited that I'm pregnant," she asked, sounding like she had picked up a bad cold in Antarctica. "What if he says he wants six kids all of a sudden?"

"If you were convinced that your marriage could survive and that Tom had just done this one time and you knew in your heart that he would never do this again, how would you feel about six kids?"

"But I'm not sure I believe the marriage will survive."

"And I'm not saying you have to know that right now. I'm saying the answers you give tonight, should be based on the marriage surviving. This is called compartmentalization. It's often very hard. I have to do it every day. In about an hour, I have to tell someone they are not getting a promotion they want. An hour after that, I will be giving someone an award. The discussion you and I are having right now will stick with me the rest of my life, yet I can't let it bleed into what I will be doing this afternoon. What Tom did, will stick with you the rest of your life. But you can't let it bleed into everything going forward. I've seen women do that. They let it pollute this marriage, then the next, and then how they raise their kids, and how they look at other women at a party. For your own sake you can't do that.

"Whether you stay married to Tom or not, eventually you will have to forgive him or it will mess you up horribly. Then you'll still probably spend the rest of your life having to forgive him every time it surfaces in your mind. The good news is that it becomes easier with time.

"So find out what it is you're forgiving and then forgive. You won't feel like it, but do it. Forgiveness is not a feeling. It's an action. It means you will simply not look for a way to hurt back. It will be the hardest thing you have ever done. But it will be the biggest thing you have ever done. If you only take one piece of advice from me today, let this be it: Forgive."

"So deal with the pregnancy issue on the assumption I'm going to stay married..."

"Yes, regardless of how the test turns out this afternoon."

14

"...and then deal with the cheating."

"Yes and then make your decision on whether you will stay married. After that, if you decide to keep going, you will work out with him how you will stay married. It's a progression. Can you handle that?"

"I think so."

"Good. Now you look a mess. Why don't you use my office for a while? I need to run back across the street. Theresa will take care of anything you need. Okay?"

"Thank you."

"And one other thing – please call Theresa after your doctor's appointment and have her interrupt me."

The test was positive. More tears. And another long talk on the phone. She called from home. She wanted to rehearse one more time. Toward the end of our talk, she came up with a good question: "What if I start crying?"

"I think if you really fear crying you are more likely to cry. Let me tell you why you should not fear crying. Are you ready?"

"Yes."

"You just found out you are going to have a baby. You're pregnant. You have tons of emotional latitude. Almost nothing you do will be considered out of the norm. You'll be fine."

"Okay. That's good."

"Let me add another complication – a good one I hope. You are now making decisions that affect someone who will arrive in about 8 months. Hopefully, that will give you some additional justification for not reacting too strongly tonight. You're not being a doormat. You're being smart. There's a lot at stake here. There are now three people who will be impacted by what finally gets decided. That's why you're taking it one step at a time."

"I'm compartmentalizing," she sniffed, repeating her lesson.

"I am so sorry that this is happening this way. But you have to believe me, it will work out and the right thing will be done. You're a good person. Life will be good again."

"Thank you."

"And one more thing: You'll be a great mom."

The night went smoothly. She was ready. He was very excited and offered to break out a bottle of champagne until he realized that it was probably not a good idea to have alcohol.

She called me the next morning.

"He wanted to take me out to dinner tonight."

"Isn't morning sickness a blessing?"

"It comes in handy. Do you mind if I take a couple days off?

"Today's Wednesday. Why don't you take three?"

"Because I want to talk about subject number two this weekend and I would really like to sit down with you one more time on Friday."

She was a different woman on Friday. She was angry. She was convinced she could raise a kid alone. And she was just fine with the idea of having only one child.

After she delivered her speech, I sat there with my eyebrows raised to the ceiling and with a look on my face like "Whoa! What was that!?"

"So, have you talked with him already?

"No."

"Did you find out some new information?"

"No."

"Then I'm glad you got that speech you just gave me out of your system so we can talk about what you really need to do." I leaned my elbows on the desk and smiled.

She tried to look away in order to keep her angry moment intact. But it didn't work. Cynthia was Cynthia. She was smart, reasonable, and open-minded. I knew she wanted to keep her marriage if it could be done without too much compromising of her dignity. And her dignity was what I had in mind when I asked her the first question.

"How do you plan to start out when you talk to him?" It was important that I let her start to feel like she was in control of how things should proceed. She would eventually be on her own and she had to feel like she was not dependent on someone else at each step. The difficulty was that in her present state, breaking such a tough problem into soluble elements was just too hard. She still needed help to avoid reflex actions.

"I'll tell him what the doctor found and that since I wasn't... since I didn't...pick it up, it was clear to me where I had gotten it. I'll say that and then I'll wait for his response. Do you think that's a good way to get it out on the table?"

"No."

"Why not?"

"Because the issue you need to deal with is his infidelity. He broke a sacred trust and that's all you focus on."

"But he's going to want to know how I know..."

"Let him wonder."

"So what do I say, 'Tom, have you been unfaithful to me?'"

"Pretty much."

"That just seems so...I don't know."

17

"Cynthia, are you certain that he cheated on you?"

"Yes."

"Is there not a huge trust issue now?"

"Yes."

"If he can't come right out and admit he has cheated, doesn't that make it worse? And conversely, if he lowers his head and confesses that he has done it and that he's ashamed, sorry and it will never happen again, won't that at least get you to the point where you want to talk about it?"

I felt that would help her create an orderly view of the conversation. But I was wrong.

"God, this is awful," she said, shaking her head. "I don't know if I even want to..."

"You can't just get off this bus and walk home, I'm afraid."

"It just... the whole thing is just..."

"Cynthia, it is what it is. All I'm trying to do is to help you get it to where it's your option. You need to be in the position to make the best decision possible, the most important decision of your life perhaps – and that of your baby's."

That woke her up.

"You're right."

We sat in silence for a few moments.

"What if he plays coy?"

"What if?" I returned.

"I don't know."

"How will you feel?"

"Like leaving him."

"I think at that point you have to tell him you know for a fact that he has been unfaithful and that his next words will determine whether you stay together or not. Then sit back, fold your arms and wait."

Blubbering like a baby, Tom confessed everything, right off.

"Did he offer you a satisfactory explanation – one that you can live with?" I asked when she returned to work, almost a week later.

"He said that he felt really lonely and that I had been working such late hours, he just got caught up in a situation he regretted. He felt that I didn't care anymore and that it seemed like I just wasn't even trying."

"What did you say to him?"

I said, 'So then, long hours and unbrushed hair cause infidelity?'"

"I think I've heard that," I said, meeting her faint, sad smile.

Cynthia and Tom worked it out because Cynthia put the ball right in Tom's court. He was to act like an adult and make her look up to him once again. To his credit, he gave it all his energy. It affected everything he did including his work. His career began to move forward after it had been stagnating for a couple of years. She knew she had her husband back.

Cynthia told me that she felt the marriage would never be what it could have been but it would still be good. I disagreed with the first part of that statement. I asked her whether she would rather have a husband that was floating along in a marriage or a husband who was working hard at that marriage every day of his life because he now valued it so greatly. She said the answer was somewhere in between her view of the future and mine.

She was probably right.

We started out this story with a definition of betrayal. It hinged on the willingness of the betraying party to devalue and hurt. Ostensibly, Tom did not intend to hurt Cynthia, nor did he mean to devalue her. But he did both, whether he set out to do so or not. It was not intentional but it's kind of like driving your car on a crowded sidewalk because you're stuck in traffic. You have no intention of hitting a pedestrian but the minute you turn that wheel and leave the road, you have to know that you're doing something wrong and you're putting others at risk. Cynthia was right in feeling betrayed.

There's an ugly, oft quoted statistic out there that can cause someone to give up on a marriage a little more easily than he or she should. You hear all the time that 50% of the marriages end up in divorce. That may be so, but that doesn't mean 50% of the people who get married, get divorced. The truth is 70% of all people who get married, stay with their spouse until death.

As a nation and as a society we firmly believe in marriage. Unfortunately, the people who have the microphone at the moment think marriage is a throwback to more primitive times or that it is an exploitative relationship. It's neither. It's a wonderful thing and worth preserving. It's not perfect and it's rarely smooth sailing. But with work, it becomes something both husband and wife can look at proudly and say, "We built that."

The fact that Cynthia's husband was willing to get back to the business of building was important. By clearly demonstrating that he valued the marriage, he showed Cynthia that he valued her. He began reversing the damage of devaluation caused by betrayal. And though the two of them would always know that the precious Ming vase that sat in their entryway had a hairline crack which only they knew about, they also knew over time that there are a lot of other issues that come up which will determine the quality of a marriage. In your thirties, sobriety sets in. Kids, finances, careers, and houses become the items on the menu. Good men settle down and settle in.

Life rolls forward and muffles the past.

Megan

She started off with a statement I had heard women hint at but never state quite so categorically – and therefore say out loud a notion that was so categorically wrong.

"I think he cares about me but I don't think he cares how I'm feeling most of the time," she proposed, as if that could potentially explain one of the disappointments she had in her relationship with her flancé. If it's explicable then maybe it's tolerable, she no doubt thought. I've seen women rationalize lousy situations. The sad thing is how often so many women have to do it.

"Megan, before I address the impossibility of such a thing as caring about you but not about how you're feeling, let me ask this. Have you ever kind of laid out in your mind what an ideal relationship would look like?"

She spent some time in generalities and then, as if to define it clearly she said, "I want one like you have with Kristy."

"Have you ever met Kristy?"

"No, but other people have talked about you two. And it's pretty clear you love her."

"Because I told little stories about Kristy at the party?"

"And the way you tell them."

She was right. I absolutely adore Kristy.

"How do you know he doesn't care how you feel?" I asked, trying to hide my view of the logic of her opening statement.

"I don't know. It's just a sense."

"People don't say something like that based on just a sense."

"I haven't really thought it through."

"Yes you have."

"I mean, I really don't have a good explanation for it all."

"Explanation for what? Why he doesn't care how you feel or why you *think* he doesn't?"

She was stuck. So I helped her.

"Think about it, Megan. Saying someone cares about you but he doesn't care about your feelings is like saying 'I really like strawberry ice cream but I don't like the flavor.'"

She smiled. I continued.

"This actually could help me," I surmised.

"How's that?"

"Well, I have a couple of friends who think I'm not cool because I don't like jazz music. Now I can say I like it."

She looked perplexed.

"Yep. I like jazz – I just hate the way it sounds. You have made me instantly cool."

I let it sink in. Then I asked, "Does he ever ask you how you're feeling?"

"Not really."

"How long have you been together? Maybe he just knows how you feel by now."

She and Tom had been together off and on for three years. He took her for granted all three years. She had recently left him for a few months. During that time, he called her a lot more and spent a fair amount of effort trying to get her back. He then proposed to her and they were together again, engaged. At that point he went back to his old self – a lump.

Prior to the proposal and not long after she had left him, she met another guy at the client's office. Zach was a lot of fun, reasonably good looking and very pleasant. They started going out and he started getting serious about her. He became aware of her longtime relationship with Tom. He was also aware that she still had feelings for Tom, even though he had been a complete jerk. She kept going back to Tom's house for brief stints. Zach got her to agree to stop seeing Tom but it didn't actually end things. After a while Zach gave an ultimatum. When she said she wanted some more time, he ended the relationship.

"It seems as though you really liked Zach and he sounds like a pretty good guy."

"He was."

"So, why didn't you cut it off with Tom?"

"It's hard to just walk away from someone after being in a relationship with him for three years."

"Okay, it's hard. That still doesn't answer the question. You had all the data you needed. You saw no improvement over the course of three years – and no attempt on his part to improve. What more do you need?"

"I just felt really bad. He was devastated when I left the first time and he really wanted me back. I hated seeing that. I know he still loves me."

"He loves you except for the fact that he doesn't care how you feel?"

She let that go past her. "We owned a car together; we had bought Emmy, our Labrador together; we had a wine collection we were building up – lot of things. It's not like he just showed up on my porch and took me out on dates for three years."

"So, walking away would devastate Tom and it would be complicated. Is that what I'm hearing you say?"

"You're hearing me say it's not a clean and clear situation. That's why I told Zach I needed the time."

"I don't think that's why. And Zach knew it. If you had said you were going to leave Tom immediately but had to clear up who got the dog and who got the Chateau Latour, I doubt Zach would have had a big problem with it. What you said to him, even if you didn't use the words, was you're not ready to let go of Tom and therefore you might still go back to him. What intelligent guy would invest in *that* relationship?"

"You see. You're painting the picture kind of like I saw it. It's very complicated."

"No, it isn't." I was starting to sense what Zach must have felt. "Let me just give you an illustration on decision making. When I came here, I reorganized the whole company. Do you remember the reaction?"

"Everybody was furious."

"Why?"

"For about 50 reasons. The salespeople were not going to have..."

"You already answered the question: there were about 50 reasons people hated my guts. By the way, something you don't know is that the former owners, who still had a stake in the business and who had just reorganized the company before I took over, also hated my guts. Do you think maybe I had a mess on my hands?"

She smiled. "I kinda hated you too."

"And now how do you feel? How would you say we are doing as a company?"

"Great."

"Did it turn out to be the right decision?"

"Yes."

"But I admit I did have a mess for a while. However, that's just the way it is with big decisions. They are never without complications. It seems like someone always gets hurt or bent out of shape. But it could have gotten even worse. Don't you think I would have altered my decision if it got a lot messier than it already was?"

"Probably."

"Nope. I would only alter my decision if I thought it was wrong. Not because it hurt. I might try to salve the pain here and there, but I would stick with it until it was clearly the wrong decision or if external things changed so much that it called for a different course of action altogether. So let me give you the rule:

'Make the decision and then clean up the mess.'"

I could see her churning over in her mind what cleaning up the mess would look like. I could tell she wasn't ready. This was not surprising. She had gotten very good at rationalizing repeated bad choices regarding Tom.

"Let me give you another rule. It's based on the fact that whenever I have had one of the executives who reports to me, come to my office with a really dumb decision, it's not because they are stupid or inexperienced or evil. It's because they are solving the wrong problem. They want to reorganize instead of dealing with a specific personnel issue. They want to launch an expensive program instead of just getting the sales people to do their jobs. The problem they are solving is avoiding the uncomfortable task of forcing the issue with their people. They often don't know which way to force it or they are dealing with people who report to them who are pretty tough and who can be pretty nasty."

"You think I'm solving the wrong problem? But it seems like there's only one problem to solve."

"Yes. You are solving the wrong problem. You are solving the problem of how to deal with the implementation once you have made your choice. Either it's right to stick with Tom or it's not. All you have to do to figure that one out is sit back and imagine being treated like he's been treating you... for the next 50 years. Does that sound appealing?"

She slowly took a deep breath and shook her head slightly, indicating she was imagining something that wasn't a whole lot of fun to be a part of.

"And do me the favor of not believing he will mellow out over time and suddenly realize what a gem you are and then start fawning all over you and putting you first before everything else in his life. It never happens with guys like that. If it was a matter of him making a big screw-up in an otherwise good relationship, that's one thing. But to me, it sounds like this guy just flat doesn't care. The early years of a relationship are when the greatest amount of infatuation occurs. Are you still waiting for that?"

"It's probably not going to happen."

"But you're not about to leap up out of your chair and say, 'By golly, I'm done!' are you?" She didn't respond. I finished my point. "Can I tell you the next wrong problem you're going to solve, just to save you a little time?"

"What's that?" she said, still lost in a bit of reflection.

"You're going to try to figure out ahead of time how you will find someone to replace Tom. You'll realize that Zach's probably out of the picture - so who else is going to come along? You'll think Tom is at least *someone.* You will try to solve the problem of how to avoid being lonely for a guy."

"I don't know. Maybe...probably."

"Don't do it. A problem tooth needs a filling. A rotten tooth needs to be pulled. Don't worry about how you're going to chew filet mignon without that tooth. You'll eventually be chewing cold mush if you leave it in."

The other wrong problem she and many women in this situation attempt to solve is *his* problem. How is *he* going to get along when she leaves him? Women tend to be monogamous and loyal. They hang in there, even when the guy is less than admirable. Tom had never really committed to Megan. She owed him civility and that's it.

Normally, women are pretty good at spotting jerks. Women have needed to have really good antennae for reasons of survival. That's why I always have at least one woman interview a guy before I hire him. It lowers my odds of hiring someone who's insincere or an outright creep that the guys and I couldn't spot. But I don't use people like Megan to do those interviews. She is one of those women who get totally fooled. They are the type of woman who marries the same type of guy over and over. He just has a different name and hair color the second and third time.

Handing back that engagement ring was one of the hardest things she ever did. She sat in my office and cried on more than one occasion.

It took less than a month before she came back to my office to tell me she felt like a huge weight had been lifted off her. She knew she had made the right decision.

A sad fact is that most women are better wives and mothers than men are husbands and fathers. This doesn't mean that men are always lousy husbands – far from it. There are a lot of great guys who are loving, devoted husbands. But the odds are high that a man won't value and nourish a marriage as much as a woman will. If this is already how it is, why would anyone want to move the odds to 100% by continuing to date a jerk?[1] He may become more responsible and earn more money. He may even settle down a bit. However, it is highly unlikely that he will put the effort into the marriage that he should. The woman will suffer. He won't care about her feelings because his come first. If he doesn't care about her feelings then he doesn't care about her. No one should sign up for that arrangement.

And don't adjust to it by dating the wrong guy so long that your skin just gets thicker because:

Jerks don't change. They just find better camouflage.

---

[1] It's important to define the word jerk, since it comes up a lot. A jerk is a self-important person who consistently puts his own interests and happiness in front of yours, he knows he's doing it and he knows it's unfair, yet he still expects you to put up with it – and maybe even think he's cool.

Sidebar: A Kristy Story

Megan mentioned the fact that I tell Kristy stories. Here is one from an email I sent out to family members and a few others:

I was working at my desk at home when Kristy informed me there was a spider in the bathroom sink. "A big wolf spider." (It wasn't a wolf spider).

I didn't think much of the news report and I didn't think it was a statement of work. So I finished the email I was writing and then wandered down the hall. Kristy was standing with her hands on her hips, staring at the spider in the sink. She mentioned that I "took long enough." She was wearing her striped, pink, evil bee shirt, to set the scene for you.

I scooped the spider into my hand and tossed it out the back door. This allowed Kristy to get on with what she was doing.

This is very sad. She was held hostage by a spider in the sink.

I went to the Internet and did a search for the most terrible things on earth. They are in this order:

1. *Starving children in Guatemala*
2. *Puppies wandering onto a busy road*
3. *People with a spider in the bathroom sink*

This is only a partial list but you see where the situation ranks.

Dad

Author's Note: The response from all the women on my distribution list was swift and nasty; not because of the insulting note, but because I took so long to go get the spider.
No matter how far we come in creating equality between the sexes, men will still be responsible for removing spiders from sinks and bathtubs.

Andrea

Every time we make a big thing out of the fact that Wendy is the first woman to ride a bicycle backwards or Sarah was the first woman to rise to a certain level in a big company, we demean women. And worse, we make them feel like it's a really, really hard thing for a woman to do – low odds – so don't bet on doing it yourself. I know it's supposed to be a statement as to how far our primitive society has come, but for heaven's sake, enough already.

My questions: Does she have all her mental faculties and does she speak reasonable English? Great. Go compete. She's not an anomaly; so let's quit making it seem that way.

Tell me about some dog that talks or a kangaroo that flies. Such creatures are not designed to do those things. A talking dog is an anomaly. A capable, committed woman succeeding in business is not.

All you angry college professors with beards and ponytails, come on out. The war's over. You won. Women won. As a culture, we all won. Let's quit talking about it.

When I came to my office, Andrea was playing with one of the knickknacks on my desk. She felt perfectly at ease wandering around my office looking at things. She had worked for me for a few years prior to that day. She left to go to a good-sized technology services firm that I and everybody else thought would be perfect for her. We parted as friends. It was good to see her because I hadn't heard from her in a long time.

"I always liked that you had little brain teaser puzzles to play with," she said, twisting at a four-inch wood lattice with a marble in it.

"So you like those puzzles?" I asked.

"No. I like the fact that *you* have them and not me. I hate 'em. You always were so good at them and you got so excited when someone gave you one." She twisted it a couple more times and then handed it to me. "Okay, so how does it work?"

"Well," I said, placing it on the corner of my desk and positioning it just right. I tapped it and squeezed it a bit. She watched intently. "It works by looking at it. It's not a puzzle."

She laughed as we both sat down.

"I feel comfortable here," she started. "I was concerned about coming back but it feels like old home week — except for the fact that I don't recognize half of the people. But it feels really relaxing to sit in your office again. I have a boss who is...let's just say...he's to the point. No wasted words."

"That's no fun," I protested. "I like wasting words. It makes me feel rich and extravagant. Besides, I like going through wasted words afterwards to see if there's anything good left over. There always is, you know."

"In a way, that kind of makes sense," she laughed. "But, you see, that's my point. My boss would never say something like that."

"Is that why you're here? Boss problems?"

"No, not so much...well...it's...no, the thing is...yeah sort of but not really."

"Well, Andrea, the good thing is that no matter what advice I give you, it probably won't be entirely wrong." We both laughed.

"I mean what the heck was that sentence? Does it have a name – like a haiku or something?"[2]

When she quit laughing she took a deep breath and nodded, smiling. "Yeah, that was pretty bad."

"No wonder he doesn't waste words," I yelped, sarcastically. "He's scared to death of what you'll do with them! Poor guy. I'll call him when we're done here and tell him everything's going to be all right."

Andrea's concern was not her boss. It's hard when you can't get close to someone after working with him for a long time, but that happens. I usually grow on people but I too have had bosses who were not personable at all. You never feel as good about yourself as you could. What a dumb way to manage.

What she was trying to figure out was how to get promoted. She actually had a chance to move to a level higher than her boss but in a different area of the company. She knew she would be a candidate when the opportunity arose. So she wanted to talk to me to help her get herself into a better position.

Women often feel that it gets kind of hardcore as you get closer to the top of the organization. They think they are really being judged thoroughly and scrutinized harshly, almost microscopically. It's scary.

Well guess what: Welcome to the club. We all feel that way.

---

[2] I just went back and counted the syllables in that awful utterance of Andrea's. I swear I didn't change it to make it fit. There are 17 syllables – just like a haiku. I'm sure there are some structural problems, however. But if you ever read a Japanese haiku, it makes about as much sense and the poetry element is probably on track as well.

Unless you're one of those few golden boys or golden girls who have been pre-selected and now all you have to do is avoid screwing up and you'll get promoted, you need to slug it out like the rest of us. It seems like every promotion I have ever gotten had less than a smooth launch and landing. It always had some glitch or delay. It was like being handed a treat just after it had been dropped on the floor. I suppose if I were a woman or minority I would be thinking that's par for the course for women and minorities. Since I'm neither, I think that's par for the course for left-handed, blonde-haired guys named Charles.

Believe me, the grass is not that much greener over here.

We always think the other person has it easier. I remember the slower guys on our high school track team thinking those of us who were fast weren't as nervous before a race. Let me tell you something, when you step up to the line to run 800 meters against some tall, sinewy guy you have never seen before, you're scared. Why would you be less scared? Your reputation's on the line. You're about to run your lungs out in a two-lap sprint. Varsity track in a big city's metropolitan league is varsity track. There aren't any slow guys! The only people who aren't scared, aren't running. They're in the stands, watching.

Andrea expressed her concerns about being worthy enough to pass muster and wanted a bit of a roadmap. To her credit, she wasn't looking for a *woman's* roadmap. She just wanted some ideas; so she had "come back home" to where she could talk freely; and hopefully get some helpful counsel.

One of the benefits I got from working in IBM headquarters was the chance to work with the Director of the Executive Resources department on a number of occasions. I was on a special assignment to a Vice President. The Executive Resources

Director was in his group. He was responsible for working with field and HQ executives to identify the people who were to move through the ranks and possibly run IBM someday. He kept the war room up to date. In many corporate war rooms in those days, you could go inside and see all the high level positions and then several names by each one. These were the candidates to fill the slot if the person presently in it left for whatever reason.

The director laid out for me the basics for what it took to get promoted. It comes down to three things: experience, success, and image. You can see how interwoven those are if you think about it for a minute. It's a combination of chicken-and-egg, mixed with rock-paper-scissors at any given time in your career. Experience tells what you did. Success tells how well you did it. Image on the other hand aims more at the future. It determines how the upper level execs view your long-term potential by how you carry yourself and react to stuff. It's the words you choose to say and the things you choose not to say. It's how hard it looks when you're trying to get something done. Are you a leader or not? It's also the sense upper management has about your charisma and your intellect. What does your image tell them about all this? They aren't going to find any of this out on some report.

You see, even if you can perform the next job up the ladder, why would anyone let you clog up that spot in a big corporation if you can't go any farther? That perhaps is the most frustrating thing to people who see themselves as well qualified for a promotion to the next *key* position. You may be. But if you're not well qualified for the next promotion plus the one after that and the one after that, why should those of us at the top waste the time promoting you? Why even get started?

This is where women often lose the race.

When an opportunity comes up for a job at the next level, women look at the job, they see what is needed to do the job and then they look at how fit *they* are to do the job – they weigh the pros and cons. This is simply not how it works.

In my book, *A Guide to Managing Earthlings*, I explain how decisions are really made. Without taking you through the entire chapter, let me summarize by saying any decision starts with a gut feel and then that gut feel is verified. Thus, your image must precede your internal resume. You can't get by without some substance and experience but that's not where it starts. I mean think about it, how many times have you seen someone who you felt was not qualified to shine your shoes get a promotion?

And this is why it angers me to hear about some woman being touted as a hero, pioneer and iconoclast for making VP at some engineering firm that is mostly made up of men. When this happens, they almost always talk about how incredibly hard she worked and how wonderfully qualified she was. I say work incredibly hard and build your credentials but spend every second of every day managing your image and how you should come across – three levels up.

Let's look at the logic in aiming just for the next level. Remember, this is for <u>key</u> positions on the way to the top (wherever that is). Here's how it goes:

> *If the promotion is dependent on you being viewed as capable of making it up the chain to higher level executive jobs in the future, and you view those jobs as for somebody else (like a guy), you will tend to aim only for the lower level job as your next resting spot. As a result, you won't act like*

someone who is ready for even higher level executive jobs. Therefore, you won't look like executive material, so you probably won't get promoted to one of the jobs that lead there.

So, why does this hurt women more than men? Two related things: a woman's honesty to the point of being her own saboteur, for one; and self-deprecation that leads to lousy self-esteem and a less than bold comportment for the other. Guys think they are better than they are. They think they ought to be the next president right now. They puff up and swagger. Some of them learn to refine their image (swagger with a bit of class) and then up the ladder they go; while women are sitting in your office telling you all their holes and why they aren't quite fit for the job you're getting them ready to move to. Who wants Eeyore running the sales department!?

Of course, you have to have talent and drive and all that but you'll never get to use it in the upper echelons if you don't have..."it" (image, confidence, panache, etc.).

Here's one other helpful way to look at it. As you move closer to the top, the placement of executives is a lot more like casting actors for a movie. Manage your image as if you want to be the leading lady. Otherwise, you will become a character actor for the rest of your career.

When Andrea started talking about the job she was after, she began by telling tell me her strengths and weaknesses and how they stacked up against the job and against the other people she thought might be in line for the job. I cut her off.

"You can do this in front of me, Andrea, because I'm a friend. Just promise me you won't do this in front of anyone in your company. This is not how they are going to evaluate you on the first pass. They will have a sense about you and then they will probe a little deeper to see if they're right. Your job is to get to the point where they are only considering *you* and only probing *you* because they have this wonderful sense about *you*. And I'll tell you right now, *you* are not coming across that way. So let's fix it."

"Fix what?"

"Your image. If you're like most people at your level, hearing this for the first time, you think that managing your image is somehow putting on a façade. But it's not, unless you consider that we are all putting on a façade almost every day on almost every subject."

"I guess I'm lost. What about my image am I supposed to be managing?"

"You are managing the image you need to have to look like you are three levels higher in the company than you are right now. What does that look like?"

"This isn't what I expected. I was looking for a few tips on what to say and not to say when interviewing and trying to get my career going. I had some ideas about the moves I wanted to make and the people I wanted to try to get on my side." Andrea was getting distressed. She was talking physics and I was talking philosophy and metaphysics. In her mind, if what I was saying is true, then she was going to have to go to finishing school for the next several years to be able to play a role in order to get promoted. I could tell she was starting to get bugged. She was looking for a good cake recipe and I was trying to give her the whole bakery. So I went directly to work on the subject of image.

"Okay, let's step back. You see I run a big operation." She nodded. "So tell me, what attribute other than some smarts do I need, in order to stay in charge and have people all around me respect me? Just pick an attribute."

"Okay, let me think. Attention to detail..."

"Yuk. That's not an attribute. Pick a good one."

"I knew that would annoy you," she smiled.

"An attribute. Boy Scout stuff," I offered as a hint.

"Trustworthy, brave, clean..."

"Courage?" I asked, with a glimmer of hope.

"Yeah, brave. Courage, I suppose," she said after giving it a little thought.

"Why? It's my favorite example - but why?"

"I don't know. I guess because everyone's always coming at you. You have to make decisions and it seems that half the people are thinking you're wrong. Lots of reasons."

"What if one of our largest accounts dumps us? I'll not only come in 30% below my target on revenue, I'll get killed on profitability because all those people on that account won't be billing. They'll be sitting on the bench and I'll still be paying them. Do you think that would be a bit scary for my career? Do you think courage might come into play? Here, let me show you something."

I pulled up an email and had her come around to the computer on my desk to read it. It was forwarded to me by one of my project executives, one of my best people. The client was planning to postpone our big project. She read it quietly and then looked at me.

"What are you going to do?"

"Before I answer that, how do you think I feel right now?"

She went back to reading the email. "I'd be sick to my stomach."

"Would you be scared?"

"Yes."

"Do you think I'm scared?"

"You don't look scared."

"Have I looked or acted scared the whole time you've been sitting here?"

"Not at all. Are you?"

"Of course, I'm scared. But if I look scared, then everyone who depends on me will know there's a serious problem and that their leader is possibly compromised with fear. Courage is not a façade. And it's not insensitivity to what might kill you. It's managing through tough times with a bit of class. It's showing you're not shaking in your boots. It's doing what needs to be done, even if you want to hide under your desk."

"So, what are you going to do?"

"We'll figure it out. If it wasn't this it would be something else. Stuff happens. And it happens all the time. Andrea, the two questions you have to answer are: Do you really want to deal with this kind of ongoing trouble? And can you do so without falling apart?"

"Yes and Yes."

"Perfect. You just passed the first test. The fundamental question your superiors have to be able to answer about you is whether you can handle it. Can you handle it emotionally, physically, intellectually, with civility, class and professionalism? Is your judgment generally sound? Do you pick your battles? Do you run off at the mouth because you're nervous and you don't feel good about yourself? This is image management. Can you do it?"

She started to give an explanation and then said, "Yes."

"Okay, so courage is looking brave when you're scared.

What does intellectual prowess look like?"

"That's a good one," she smiled. "But I know you've got to have some smarts."

"More important, you've got to show it. And even more important than that, you can't let 'em see that you might not have it under some circumstances. No holes. So how do you show it?"

She took a deep breath, concentrating hard. I interrupted.

"Come on, Andrea, loosen up. There's a bunch of these."

"I'm stumped."

"Well, if emotional strength is looking brave when you're scared to death, what is intellectual strength?"

"Looking smart when you feel dumb," she beamed.

"There you go. Now you know my number one trick. I feel like ordering a round of beers."

"But let's face it, Charles, you're not stupid or even close."

"Oh, really? Andrea, I am constantly stumped – at least momentarily. But I know that either I will figure it out, someone I put on it will figure it out, or I'll make a pretty good stab at it, see where I'm wrong, and *then* figure it out."

"That makes sense."

"Can you do it?"

"Yeah."

"One of the keys is to reject little tests that people throw at you for immediate resolution. Always have a way to buy yourself time. Once you get good at that, you'll be okay. Unless…"

"Unless what?" she fidgeted a little.

"Unless you really can't eventually figure it out and that happens too often. You have to be right on the big decisions more often than not. You'll have some blind spots. That's why you surround yourself with great people.

"Now let me combine the two you've just learned. Imagine you're a general. A messenger comes into your command tent when you're there with your general staff as the campaign against a vicious enemy rages. The messenger runs up to you without even saluting and says, 'General, those battalions you sent around the far ridge to hit the enemy from the side, they got ambushed, all 50,000 of them are dead!'"

"And I'm the general that did *that*?" Andrea asked.

"You are her. What do you say?"

"Oops."

She was joking but I couldn't ask for a better response.

"That's it!" I yelled. "You passed the test!"

She looked at me askance. "The general just got 50,000 men killed by a bad decision he made and he says, 'Oops'?"

"Darn near."

"And I get an A for *that*?" she said, doubtfully with a tinge of disgust.

"No. You get an A minus. Here's what you say, 'Okay, so the flanking maneuver didn't work and I have 50,000 fewer troops. Let's try running the 1st division up the center and...'"

I paused mid-sentence and watched her think it over.

"Andrea, what was your first instinct? You just got a bunch of fine young men killed who trusted you. You just got bested by your enemy in a key battle at the start of the campaign. Your direct reporting generals may have advised against it. Word's going to spread. How should you feel?"

"Awful, horrified, I'd want to run for the hills. I'd want to go home and go out to dinner and quit fighting wars."

"A guy would have said he wanted to go home and go fishing after killing 50,000 people but that's okay. So you feel rotten. How do you show it?"

She sat back in her chair and looked me up and down. Then she leaned forward and said, "Oops."

"Perfect! I'm proud of you. You don't say you're so sorry you could throw up. You don't say "Oh, this is so awful I'll write a letter to all 50,000 parents..."

"I think that's closer to a hundred thousand parents," she interjected with a smile. "But I get it."

"It really comes down to one word, Andrea."

"Oops?"

"Almost," I smiled. "The word is cool. You keep your cool. You're in control. You don't have to confess your inadequacies ahead of time just because you don't want everyone to be angry when they find out how dumb you really are. We're all dumb in places. Just relax. Can you do that?"

"Of course I can. If guys can do it. I can do it."

"But it will be a bit harder for you than it is for most guys."

"Why?" she said with some distress.

"Because there is just a bit of hot air in this process. And most guys are born with a lot of hot air and room for a lot more. Many of them flunk out because when they realize they have built their career on too much hot air, they lose confidence. Once your confidence starts to flag, it's good-bye career ladder.

"So, show some class; hide your fears; and take on some challenges that get you noticed. Treat people right; focus on the big stuff, talk about the big stuff. Only meet with your bosses on the big stuff. Don't get caught up in the little stuff. That way you won't get hurt by the little stuff. You also won't be known as a 'little stuff' person."

As I said, Andrea came looking for a recipe for the next few steps in the process, but I gave her a formula for the rest of her career. She needed to figure out what the people look like who are several levels up and then look like them. One other minor disadvantage for women is the fact that there aren't as many role models in higher places to pattern after. But that's going to be fixed over time as more women move into leadership roles. In the meantime, my advice to women is to avoid acting like a bunch of the men who are a bit higher in the organization than you and who are full of hubris and nastiness.

The failure to adopt a good role model hurt Hillary Clinton in her campaign for president. When she was subdued and intro-spective, working through the issues, she was a powerhouse. When she got up at a rally and started shouting and pumping her fist like some guy with a straw hat in the 1920s, she came across as fake, not energetic. She was playing a guy's game. Do you think Margaret Thatcher or Indira Gandhi ever shouted in a gravelly voice and pumped their fists? It's not how a woman is going to look like a leader, yet that's what a lot of women do.

Oops.

The fact that women often approach the difficult subject of promotion from a different angle than men has never really impacted my own decision to promote them. I have usually had more women managers at any given time than men. When a woman I'm trying to promote is self-deprecating to a fault, I just put my foot in the small of her back and shove her into her new office. I don't care much about what her shortcomings are. I want her there for her strengths. And I don't really care how she meets her objectives. I assume it will be different from the way I would do it. She also has to treat her employees well and help develop them for future opportunities.

It's clear that a lot of the women who work for me talk to me when they have problems that may or may not have anything to do with the job. The fact that I am often privy to some personal problems doesn't affect a woman's chances to move up. It would be utterly unfair to penalize them for asking for help. I know that women deal with tough emotional issues all the time. But they are used to keeping them separate from work, most of the time. In the long run, those problems rarely affect job performance.

Women are troubled mostly by the type of manager who focuses on *how* people perform their jobs instead of *what* they are able to accomplish. Everybody is troubled by "how" guys. But women in particular are, because such managers are typically accustomed to *how* they and other men operate.

How is appropriate only when the person being managed is becoming counterproductive; i.e. driving everybody crazy.

Epilogue

Andrea got the promotion but it took three months.

The game playing began as soon as Andrea's boss realized that Andrea was a real contender for a job outside of his organization. She carried herself confidently and well. He responded by going from being his laconic self to an artificially friendly guy. Andrea was onto him. He suddenly looked small and acted small. She realized how much she didn't want to be trapped working for him.

His next maneuver was to try to put her into a leadership position on a large and critical client project. At first, this was okay with Andrea since it would give her visibility and the chance to manage dozens of people. It didn't take long for Andrea to realize she would be on the Titanic. The reason there was an opening was because her predecessor had "dodged a bullet." He chose to leave before he got fired. Andrea's boss knew this.

Andrea called me and asked me what to do. I told her to refuse the assignment. She had nothing to lose by refusing it and a lot to lose by boarding a ship destined for the Atlantic floor.

By this time, Andrea had established herself with executives in the other operation within her company. Nervous as she was, she kept her cool. She was aided by the fact that she was willing to quit rather than get stuck in a losing situation. This made her come across as even more cool. She made some polite demands. Had they not been met, she would have remained employed until she found a job elsewhere. As it was, they wanted to hang onto this pleasant but steely-eyed executive.

Here's a secret rule: The guy who promotes you is almost never your boss. Why should he voluntarily agree to lose a good resource? So don't spend all your time working on him. Just make sure he can't trip you up. It's your boss's boss that typically makes the call. *That's* whom you subtly impress. But don't do an obvious end-around maneuver.

Here's another rule - an ancient rule: The best way to bargain is with your hand on the doorknob. Just don't do it every time.

Sidebar: Getting to Executive Row

Moving up the corporate ladder is not easy for anyone unless your dad owns the company. It takes work, planning, a bit of luck, and of course success along the way. Applying the Golden Rule helps too. You'd be surprised at who gets to vote informally and how one little comment can possibly derail you – at least for a while. You don't want someone who is a casualty of one of your campaigns to undermine you.

The reason some of us make it and some of us don't is almost entirely a result of our own actions and comportment. But whether you believe that or not, you have to plan and operate like it's true. If a person doesn't believe in himself or herself, that person will not carry themselves right and will be afraid to take the necessary actions to get there. Another thing that can hurt you is to focus on things you simply cannot change – such as your race or gender.

It's often somewhat easier for men to get promoted than it is for women. But even if it were ten times harder, it would still make no sense to dwell on it. So, manage your performance and manage your image. You'll get there if you want to.

As I say, it's hard for everybody.

Susan

She had attempted to reach out to me twice before but then thought better of it.

"Do you ever have those moments where it seems like things just keep getting harder and harder?" she asked, with a weak smile that must have burned 90 calories getting the corners of her mouth to turn up. We had just finished a meeting and I noticed she took a bit long to push in her chair and gather her papers together while the others left. When I looked like I was going to engage, she hesitated and then made her way to the door.

A week later she was in my office again going over a report that wasn't due for another week. She wanted to make sure it was what I wanted before she put the finishing touches on it. Again, she spoke balefully about her outlook for the future. Even *I* wanted to jump off a bridge.

She left but I now sensed she would be back soon and she would bring quite a cargo with her.

But I was wrong. It was almost three months before she spoke to me about anything but business. Then, one afternoon, we were finishing a meeting and she seemed happy enough; but then she made this comment, "Do you ever look way down the road and realize the things you always hoped for are likely never going to come your way?"

This was too much. It was the third time. These had been calls for help. I excused myself for a moment and then asked Theresa if she could move my next meeting out a couple of hours. Closing the door, I sat down, put my elbow on the desk, and placed my chin in my hand. We stared at one another for several seconds.

She finally broke her gaze. Looking down, she shook her head. I was the first to speak.

"Whenever I'm feeling that way, Susan, I purposely *don't* look down the road because I know my vision isn't right and it will screw up my outlook for a while. I guess I'm the eternal optimist and I know that even if I can't see it, there will be a better day. Obviously you're not feeling that way. How come?"

Susan had been divorced for five years. She was 38 or 39. I didn't know for sure but I knew she was approaching 40. How I knew is kind of interesting. A few months earlier, my wife and I had bumped into her and her boyfriend at that time at a restaurant. We talked for about ten minutes and then went our separate ways. A week later she was in my office.

"You didn't like Jake did you?" she more or less demanded.

"Well I ..."

"You thought he was a jerk, didn't you?"

"So how long have you been seeing him?"

"I'm not seeing him anymore. You thought he was a jerk, didn't you?"

"Are you done for good with him?" I asked, clinically.

"Done. Done. Done," she declared.

"Then I will tell you, I thought he was surface-level and insincere. I was wondering why he wasn't wearing lizard-skin hip huggers. I mean, yuk, Susan. What were you thinking?"

"I'm thinking what everyone knows: A woman over 40 has a better chance of getting hit by lightning than she does of getting married. What do you expect me to do?"

"I think it would be better to get hit by lightning than to marry a guy like Jake."

"It's just that..."

"The next time a guy like Jake asks you out, wait for a really rainy, thundery day and then go out and hang onto a tall metal flagpole."

I was seeing things in Susan lately that I didn't feel good about. She was coming in later and later. She had developed a tendency to snap at people and overall she was very negative. Nothing was good enough for her, including her own work. But the biggest concern was the amount of time she sat at her desk doing absolutely nothing.

So that day when I asked her why she had zero optimism, she resumed the pose I had been seeing now for several weeks. She just stared. So I did what I always do - ask questions that are a little out of the ordinary but always open-ended.

"Tell me what it's like getting up in the morning," I asked, settling back in my large leather chair, letting her know I had all the time in the world.

"Well, to give you an idea, I now set my alarm at least an hour earlier than I used to."

"Why's that?" I didn't tell her that it didn't add up, since she was coming to work at least an hour *later*.

"Because it just takes that much extra time to get the covers off and get up. I sometimes have to talk myself into swinging one leg out and then the next. That can take forty-five minutes or more. Then I sit up. Half the time I flop over and just lay there again. I guess I'm just really tired."

It didn't have anything to do with being physically tired.

I felt really bad for Susan. She was smart and funny and very attractive. She probably knew she was a "good catch" for the right guy – for any guy. But she was stuck, like so many women. And to be approaching 40 made it harder in two ways. First, too many men her age are targeting younger women. That's just the way it often works. Second, by the time you reach your mid-thirties, you realize that 80% of the men are either jerks or they don't act very manly, making it slim pickings and low odds. If I may toss in a third, by now you know that a man who's a bit of a jerk is not going to change. The old saying becomes true:

Men marry women hoping they will never change – and then they do.

Women marry men hoping they will change – and then they never do.

Increasingly, Susan also did what so many women do, she made self-deprecating remarks aloud. She would say she looked awful or a dress made her look fat or her last haircut was a disaster. Women do this because they think everybody else is thinking it and they want to say it before you do, which would really be painful. It would make it all too real when they were kind of hoping it wasn't true. That sounds convoluted but...

Here's an observation:

Being a woman is a lot less *being* than it is *navigating*.

It seems like women never get a rest. So they filter reality when it comes to viewing themselves. Verisimilitudes are like little benches on a steep climb. Women need them now and then to catch their breath. Empirical truth is not an appropriate metric; but I'm not sure what is.

The next question caused her to think for a moment.

"Assuming that the lens through which you are seeing the world isn't exactly clear, what color is it?" Her answer was all over the place and none of the colors were from the rainbow.

Everything pointed to her being clinically depressed. I once had an employee, an Englishman, who moved here from Manchester and became seriously depressed within six months. He told me about a time he was riding the bus on the way to work. It was during the heavy part of the commute and traffic was stalled. He remembered talking to himself and being very angry about the fact that traffic was horrible; it had been horrible for years and since nobody was really willing to do anything about it, it was going to be horrible for years to come. His feelings were so disturbingly dark that he was fortunately able to realize that something was wrong within him. He had SAD (Seasonal Affective Disorder) caused by Seattle's northerly latitude, compounded by our gray skies that persist from October thru April. When he told me about it, he said "the world just went black."

Susan's recent negativity combined with her difficulty getting up in the morning indicated she really ought to be seeing a doctor. It turned out, she had been. She was now on Zoloft and she felt it was helping a little but not enough. She had been seeing a psychiatrist up until recently but she wasn't getting anyplace in her opinion. Because of this – medicine combined with analysis getting nowhere, she was starting to feel like a lost cause. In retrospect, I could see the track that she had been making as she slid into despair. Now she was reaching out to me and possibly other people.

On a summer hike in the Wasatch Mountains my hiking buddy and I got seriously lost. We figured our best way out was to get up to a better elevation and see which way it was to the valley. To get up high, we had to climb through about a quarter mile of loose shale. We had been climbing and slipping and climbing and slipping for about a half hour when we looked over at one another and started laughing at the futility of the effort. We thought we had gained maybe 50 feet in elevation. The truth is we had no markers, so we really couldn't tell.

I think depression is like that. It takes a huge amount of energy to keep struggling upward and without a breakthrough you have no way of knowing if you're getting anywhere. It's almost as if someone you trust needs to tell you. Susan trusted me but I was not about to tell her what I really thought – that she was about 50 feet lower on the shale slide.

By the way, back in the Wasatch Mountains, we eventually made it up to the top by tacking back and forth at an angle instead of clawing away at the shale in front of us. At each point where we turned and angled up in the opposite direction, we built a two-foot shale hoodoo so we could look back and know how far we were getting. It was a great psychological lift to look down and see a dozen hoodoos. Then we came up with a plan to conserve energy. One of us would tack at an angle, get up about 50 feet and toss a rope. He would then plant himself and the next guy would grab the rope and work his way up with a lot less effort. Bottom line, we needed a new plan and a useful change of direction; we needed to see our progress; and we needed each other.

On my drive home after talking to Susan, I reflected on all the times I had heard people undergoing professional analysis and how hit and miss it was. I formulated a theory which I have since applied several times. It was based on something I learned in a college physiology class when we were talking about brain chemicals. When you are happy, the brain produces chemicals which cause you to smile. Smiling is a natural phenomenon, unique to humans. We don't learn it. It is innate. Even blind babies smile.

The interesting finding was that when you force your face into the shape of a smile, many of those same chemicals are produced, even if you are not all that happy. Some people have proposed a sort of "smile therapy" where you smile your way back from depression. Good luck with that one. It may get you out of a momentary bum mood but it is not going to fix a bio-chemical phenomenon like depression – especially if there is something that is going on in your life that is helping fuel that depression. It sounded like something from the 70's.

My strategy was not as jejune as "smile therapy." Here's how it worked:

When Susan came back to my office, I asked her about her routine at home. She acknowledged it had changed drastically and had become a dysfunctional bunch of to-dos, fits and starts, based purely on expediency. This wasn't helping her any. And the psychiatrist wasn't making much progress helping her, as far as she could tell.

Here is the fundamental difference between two approaches taken by psychiatrists and some counselors I have known.

Most professional counselors, including psychiatrists are often working to fix your mind so that your behavior will improve.

The approach I like, in non-clinical situations, says fix your behavior, even artificially, and your mind will begin to heal. With a healed mind, you will then begin to lead a normal life.

The use of the word "artificial" could be mistaken as phony, but it's not the same. It really means you do things you normally do but haven't been because you haven't felt like it. <u>And</u> you do them even if you don't see the immediate *need* to do them. Under normal mental circumstances, we all do lots of things that we don't want to do right then. We brush our teeth when we would rather go to bed; we vacuum when the carpet is only starting to get visibly dirty; we make a phone call to a parent or friend we haven't spoken to in a while, when we would rather just watch television. But when you're depressed, you don't feel like doing *anything*. As a result, at the end of each day, you look back and see hardly any progress and you know you didn't do what you should have done. You were feeling unproductive; now you feel guilty. Your sleep suffers and the next day you have less energy and even less inclination to expend what energy you do have on mundanities. It's like Monday every day of the week. You have got to break the cycle.

Force yourself to lead a normal life. Get up when you're supposed to. Do your dishes, pay your bills, and go to bed at the right time. Look back at what your daily routine was when you were functioning normally and recreate it even though the dark clouds are still there. Your mind is an amazing mixture of physiology, instinct, and your recorded experiences. It knows how to fix itself in all but abnormal circumstances. I always suggest someone see a doctor. Susan, fortunately, already had the medication acting as a safety net but what she now needed was a springboard, even one that wasn't all that springy.

She agreed to try and make her life more normal. Before she left my office that day, I asked her a couple of questions that had to do with her future expectations for life in general. I wrote down her answers.

There was no bright line indicating when the depression was no longer such a big part of her life. But we all noticed a gradual improvement. And the best part was that she did too. This in itself gave her hope. She told me that getting up in the morning became easier the day after we spoke about living her normal routine. She no longer lay there each morning with the notion that she was to get out of bed to take on another miserable day. Now, she was getting out of bed simply to stay in her routine. It was an end in itself instead of the beginning of a long hard journey. She viewed her very first act of the day as an accomplishment. When she stood up, she instantly sensed a faint glimmer of hope. She eventually reset her alarm because she didn't need that extra hour to pull the covers off and stand up. As a result, she was getting more sleep.

We talked about getting a spiral notebook. This gave her a little diary by default. She made notes to herself about how she was feeling. Her spiral notebook was full of "hoodoos."

The other piece of advice I gave her that day was to find someone besides me to help now and then. It wouldn't be wise for me to take on some extended rescue effort even though I feel good when I do it. It's part of a deeper instinct which goes back to our distant tribal roots - in the days when we helped one another because that's what you do to keep the village alive. But mostly... that's what you do.

This approach of fixing the behavior to heal the mind actually works better with women than it does with men. Women have more detailed and identifiable routines. When they return to them or tighten up their routines, they almost immediately get better. It usually seems to work.

When she had clearly turned the corner, I subtly snuck in the questions I had asked her before about future expectations. They were completely different and considerably more upbeat. I then summarized her responses, reminding her of the day I had asked the questions. She knew she was on the right path.

I think it's important to have done something to make things better than just to have them *get* better. I think it's even better than a psychiatrist getting you to realize you were smacked around too much when you were a kid. It's really hard to go back and rectify the past or even recent occurrences that you feel are particularly hurtful. Many people, myself included, went through a very rough childhood. But I am who I have chosen to be and what happened then was just something that changed the little street map of life. It didn't change the vehicle.

Susan moved to be closer to her family and closer to the sun in the Southwest. I never heard from her again. I don't know if she remarried, but I trust she's doing well.

Some Men in My Office
Regarding Two Women I Never Met and One I Did

Almost every manager spends a lot of time talking to people about both business and personal issues. The key is to make sure, when you are managing on the business side of things, you are focusing on performance and not personalities. But there is a big difference between separating personal feelings from performance issues versus being impersonal across the board.

Being a naturally garrulous person, the conversations in my office ranged from sports, hobbies, high fashion, cooking, and home remedies on the chitchat side to issues of addiction, grief, and marital problems on the more serious side. I dealt with far more of the latter than the average manager. The deeper, more serious conversations were usually with women but I had my fair share of heavy discussions with men as well.

I'm picking three such situations because they are more or less in the same subject arena – that of husbands who are disappointed with wives or indifferent to the needs or feelings of their wives, or both. This is not to say that there weren't other "women"-related issues. Two people I considered good friends and who were great husbands, talked to me a couple of times about dealing with pornography. It seems it doesn't take much for it to become a permanent addiction. This was pre-Internet. I'm sure they are still struggling. Knowing how addicting it is, a number of men in my general circle, myself included, have never logged onto a porn site on purpose. Those who have, often claim they are doing it out of curiosity. I don't believe it. Not for a second. In addition to being addicting, it disrespects your wife.

However, I cannot say that I never logged onto a porn site. I once was talking to a couple of the women on my administrative staff about opening an office in Texas. Issues of tax reporting came up. I had already had this discussion with my business partner, so I simply logged onto the Federal government site while they looked over my shoulder. The only error I made was that I typed .com instead of .gov. It was a porn site set up to take advantage of such errors. We all instantly got an anatomy lesson. That was... an uncomfortable moment, if I may be permitted to make a trauma-blocking understatement.

At one time, 60% of the revenue on the Internet was porn-related. I don't know what it is now but it's pervasive. It is a very sad statement about our culture.

Back to wife issues: Here are three short vignettes about women that I dealt with through their husbands.

Steve was a good manager and a good leader. He was from another IBM division and almost at peer level with me. He and I interacted a lot and I very much enjoyed his company at work. He was good at his job. Until one day in September, I never realized he was a lousy husband – and probably always had been.

He and I were friends at work but never saw one another socially. He had another friend at work named Dave who was also a friend of his off the job. I had known Dave since my twenties. He was about ten years older than me. Via separate routes, we had both made many moves with IBM and we were now "back home" in Seattle as our last stop.

Dave wanted to know where the Bible stood on husbands and wives. The conversation went like this:

"So, Charles, what does the Bible say about a man having authority over his wife?"

"Have you read it?"

"No."

"So I could tell you anything and you might believe me."

That caught him a little off guard. Then he thought better of it. "Yes. Yes I would Charles. So if you want to twist The Lord's words around for whatever purpose, then I'll probably go for it." The Lord's words? When did he start talking like that!?

"Dave, why do you suddenly think I'm a Bible guy?"

"Aren't you?"

"I may or may not be. Are you thinking because I don't drink and swear and tell dirty jokes that I'm a Bible guy?"

"Pretty much."

"What if I told you I have a glass of wine, now and then? Would it effectively sever the link between me and God and kinda weaken my authority as the Bible guy?"

No amount of lighthearted repartee was going to loosen him up. So I changed course a bit. "Why don't we make sure of what we're talking about and then see if this is a Biblical issue. Are you okay with that?"

He proceeded to tell me that he and his wife had been fighting like cats and dogs.

"Over what?" I asked. Dave got along with everyone.

"Stupid stuff. She's always irritable and then I get irritable. I have absolutely had it."

"Is this something new?"

"Sort of. Well, not really. It's been going on for about three years and now it's getting a lot worse. That's why I'm thinking such serious thoughts as..."

"Separating? I asked.

The question made him so utterly uncomfortable he started fidgeting. Just hearing someone say the word aloud probably made him sober up real quick. He was talking stupid.

"If your wife stopped being irritable and the fights stopped, would you leave her?"

"No."

"Then if you *did* leave her now, it would be on the grounds of irritability? How does that sound coming out of my mouth?"

It sounded beyond stupid and he knew it.

He was trying to get me to do his homework so he could go back to his wife, *who actually had read the Bible*, and tell her that this behavior was strictly forbidden by God. I convinced him that was desperately dumb, a dumb way to use the Bible, and probably not what God had ever intended. He admitted it was a knucklehead idea and we both joked about it. He left in slightly better spirits than he came in, but I could tell he was still frustrated.

He came and talked to me a few more times over the course of just a couple of weeks. Each time we talked he got more and more mellow. It turns out that when the kids left for college, he and his wife had different plans as to how to spend the extra time and freedom they now had.

He started going to Steve's place a lot and taking off on weekend fishing trips. He was having a grand old time.

His wife on the other hand wanted to spend more time with him. She was always suggesting places to go that he thought were domestic and boring. This bugged him. He let her know it and gradually the fights began and got worse.

"Does she have any friends she spends a lot of time with?"

This really hit home. He had moved five times with IBM and she had never really made a close friend. Dave had his friends at work, she had the kids. At about the time she found someone who shared her interests, Dave would walk in the door and tell her they were being transferred. When Kristy and I were moving around with IBM, we never stayed more than two years in any location and then it was on to the next promotion. Dave had pretty much done the same tour. As a result, his wife's focus was inward – toward the family and her husband.

I walked him back through his last few stops on the IBM tour and after about an hour, he realized that *he* was his wife's best friend – or at least had been. When the kids went to college, she wanted to spend time with her best friend. He wanted to spend time with *his* best friend – Steve.

"Dave, she has worked her tail off for you and the family while you focused on your career. Based on what I'm hearing, she never nagged you. She moved and moved and moved and resettled and took kids in and out of new schools and now you want to prove to her she needs to behave? Why don't you go home tonight and look into her tired, middle-aged eyes and see what's there. I'm going to guess that if you really let yourself think about it, it will rip your guts out. I'm not going to get into the psychology of it all, but I'm going to guess that she is reaching out to you any way she can to try to get you to spend time with her and say you value what she did for you and what she gave up for you – like her whole life."

Dave broke down in my office. Lots of tears. He loved his wife but over the years he had pretty much gotten used to the fact that she puttered around the house and did things and always seemed to be just fine with it. In his mind, she was the one who had gone from Jekyll to Hyde, not him. He went home and started over on the life they now had as empty-nesters.[3]

I learned a bit about Steve in the course of those conversations with Dave. On the domestic front, he was a man's man. This is sometimes the code name for a jerk. But for reasons of confidentiality, I couldn't talk about what I had heard from Dave when Steve came by my office one afternoon. Besides, on that visit Steve was already not happy with me.

"It appears your guilt-trip séance with Dave was a success," he said, half smiling.

"Did Dave talk to you about our discussions?"

"He did indeed. It kinda sounds like..."

"Good. Then you probably have all the information he wanted you to have. He and I just chatted about stuff. So, what's going on with you?"

"Less and less," he said tersely. He really didn't like me changing the subject so abruptly. "And whether you'd like to talk about it or not, I thought I should just let you know that Dave was just starting to enjoy life again and you made him feel that weekends should be spent vacuuming and spraying weeds. Did anyone ever tell you life isn't very long? And for a middle-aged guy, it's about half as long, by definition."

"Steve, you've got me at a disadvantage because of the fact that I can't really talk much about Dave. But I don't want to sit

---

[3] I later informed Dave that he should enjoy this time while it lasts. When he retires and starts messing up her routine all morning and then asks her to make him a sandwich, she'll kick him back out of there. *She'll* drive him to Steve's place.

here and have you pound on me. Dave's a big boy. He made some decisions and could probably use some encouragement right about now. But I'll leave that up to you. What can I say?"

"You know, my wife and I have worked things out to where we don't both have to go to the grocery store together every time and we can each actually do something we like and it may not be what the other person wants to do. Can you imagine?" he snorted sarcastically.

"I still feel like you're pounding on me."

"No, I'm just trying to tell you that your Ozzie and Harriet version of life is only one of many alternatives for a couple. However, it's the TV version we were all raised on, so when you tell a guy like Dave that he's being a bad Ozzie, then he feels guilty and gets in line."

He said it in such a snotty, snide way that I finally decided to defend myself. So I asked, "Did you share with him the way you and Tara approach things?"

"I was a bit late. You had already gotten to him."

"Are you happy with your arrangement?"

"It gets better every year."

"How would Tara answer that question?"

"What's it to you?"

"I don't know. You're the one who came in here and told me I'm all messed up and you used yourself and Tara as prima facie evidence. I guess I look at marriages as a two-person deal. Dave probably does too. If it's a great deal, it's gotta be great for both of you. I'm just interested to know how this 'separate but equal' approach suits the female half of the deal."

Steve went into all the things that Tara does on weekends. It sounded dreary.

67

"So, she cleans and gardens and gardens and cleans and gardens." I held up my hand, saying the words as I counted her activities on my fingers. "Wow, she does five things."

"I wasn't trying to give you an exhaustive list."

"You succeeded. Do you and Tara talk very much?"

He stood to leave. "Look here, Sigmund Freud, Dave may like this kind of garbage but I'm a little old for it. Okay?" He walked to the door. "And for your information, and this is something you'll discover over time, women become less 'chatty' as they get older. They grow up, just like we do."

"It sounds like Tara has simply accepted her lot in life. And that's what you're recommending Dave to do to his wife?"

Steve instantly bristled and told me what I could do with my little assessment, then left my office. It was a long time before he came back again for personal chats.

I had in fact crossed the line. But he had come at me belligerently, just the way Dave had described the way Steve sometimes went at Tara. Communication was initiated mostly out of irritation with her and it was often delivered to her with sarcasm. I hate it when guys act like that. They force their wives to live a gray life and then they confuse complacency with contentment. They are nicer to their dogs than they are to their wives. When you reach the sarcasm stage, the relationship is essentially in a coma.

But, I admit, I showed borderline judgment.

The third guy's story takes just a little prep.

People thought I had a very healthy diet. They seemed to ignore the fact that I had a perpetual craving for chocolate - so much so that I permitted my employees to write them off as office supplies if they would leave them on their desk for other people (mostly me) to have access to them. I particularly liked the plastic M&M man that sat on Richard's desk. A pull of his (the M&M man's) arm and out came a handful of M&Ms. I drained it on a regular basis.

Still, I ate mostly very healthy things and I was thin and fit. People often asked what I did to stay thin. I would tell them, "Don't eat bread. Don't eat cereal." At that point they realized that I had essentially told them to starve to death, since there is almost no other food at their grocery store, evidently. One guy tried it for a while but maintained his spare tire without any decrease in diameter or even tread depth. He finally told me he gave up on my nutty plan because it had made no difference.

It turned out that when he gave up bread, he doubled down on pizza, deciding that the pizza crust being unfluffy was not really bread.

"What about cereal?" I asked him.

"Gone. Don't touch it," he snorted. "All I have is oatmeal!"

"So if you have to cook a cereal grain before you eat it instead of pouring it out of a box, then it isn't cereal?"

Another reason a number of people whom I didn't really know came to talk to me was because the food editor for the Seattle Times newspaper often called me for input on healthy eating in general. My name appeared occasionally in the paper.

Many of the conversations I had with others at work were with those people who were honestly concerned with their health or their weight. But my conversation with Glen took an interesting turn and got more personal. He was actually there because of concerns about his *wife's* weight. It reminded me of the Jeff

Foxworthy observation: "When women get depressed, they say, 'I'm fat.' When men get depressed they say, 'My girlfriend's fat.'"

I had seen Glen's wife. She was about 50 years old, attractive, and at most she was 3 ounces overweight.

I sat there and listened as Glen told me that he was becoming increasingly distraught over the fact that his wife was picking up a few pounds and "losing her figure." He said it was particularly hard when he is surrounded all day by women who *do* "keep themselves up."

He was about 15 years older than me but I kind of knew what was going on in his head. So I asked him for some examples of women around him who were doing much better than his wife at staying svelte. All the women he listed were in their late twenties or early thirties. None of them was in much more, if at all, better shape than Glen's wife. What Glen was dealing with were two things: a man's natural interest in other women and a man's common tendency to prefer a 28 year-old over a 50 year-old. It is the job of all husbands to arrest such proclivities; and it's important not to even start that eye wandering. I told him so. I told him he was putting pressure on his 50 year-old wife to look and act 30 years old. It's just flat unfair. There's nothing wrong with a woman *wanting* to look more youthful but to have the perpetual sense that she is not living up to her husband's expectations if she doesn't, is cruel.

He didn't like that and told me that I would feel differently in another ten years.

I said, "Maybe so. I don't know. But I can tell you one thing, when my wife is 50, I'm going to let her be 50."

Staying really fit and healthy is something I would always encourage, regardless of someone's age. But I don't think telling someone to look like Malibu Barbie is either healthy or nice. Let her move on. Men need to ratchet down their appetites and shift their focus, just a bit. Sex is a big part of marriage in the early years and then it tapers off. A man shouldn't let his mid-life crisis become his wife's raison d'être.

And by the way, when she's 55, let her be 55. This also extends a ways in the other direction to 45, 40...

Some Men in My Office

Sidebar: Men Sharing the Load
(and another Kristy story)

Kristy and I had been married for three days when I decided to clean the bathroom in our little apartment. I always got up early. The bathroom needed a little Comet cleanser here and there, so why not?

Later, I was sitting on the couch reading when Kristy came and sat down near me. "I would have done that," she said solemnly, eyes lowered.

"Done what?"

"Cleaned the bathroom."

"Well, I did it. Now you don't need to."

"But I would have, it was just that..."

"Wait a second. Are you thinking that the reason I cleaned the bathroom was to make a statement – that I was letting you know you had waited too long?" I had a look of astonishment on my face. I also had a great big smile. She was awfully cute.

Kristy and I were an old-fashioned couple in the sense that we didn't live together before we got married. I found out later that in her family, women did all the household chores. The dad and the boys did little, including cook. When Kristy was 16, her mother died. Kristy then did all the household chores plus work at McDonald's to help support the family during a tough time – all while she was a fulltime high school student.

I, on the other hand, was raised in a strict English household. No drinking before 5. When a woman who was a guest left the table or sat back down, you stood up. And you left a room better than when you came in. My brother and I did as many house-hold chores as my sister.

73

These days, I'm always up for a couple of hours by myself. I often go to the track and workout at 5 AM. When I come back, I make myself breakfast, do the dishes, and clean up the kitchen.

Kristy vacuums and mops. She probably does 60+ percent of the daily chores. I do bigger jobs when they come up - clean the roof, build stuff, change the oil and fix cars, etc.

I tried doing laundry every once in a while to help save her some time. However I stopped. Here's why.

I would start putting things in the washer and she would show up to watch me, her skinny little arms folded, peering around at the piles I sorted and occasionally moving things from one pile to another.

She would then come over and stand next to me while I tossed the last items into the washer.

"I never wash these with those other things," she would say as she fished something out of our front-loader. "And these will lose their elastic, so they should be done in cold water or by hand."

"Okay, I'll remember that," I would say, as I started to close the door to the washer.

"And always zip this up," she said, rescuing a small sweater. "It keeps it from getting beat up and ruining the shape."

"Anything else?" It appeared she was done. But...

"That's way too much detergent. You only need about half of that. And don't use too much bleach on these. And..."

"Thanks, I'm really glad I could help save you some time."

Later, I would go into the laundry room to find everything folded and the next load washing.

Men can share and they should share. But it appears there are limits and boundaries we are not always aware of.

74

Darcy

Darcy and I had been part of a batch of IBM trainees that came in during a fairly large wave of hiring. When I was hired, the Carter recession was still going. IBM Seattle had room for one new hire. I somehow got the job. A few more trickled in several months later; but then for some reason the floodgates opened and 10 new IBM trainees were hired. They joined our division which sold the very large mainframe computers with price tags of tens of millions of dollars for a complete system.

Darcy was hired into systems engineering. All sales had a technical component and the systems engineers were needed to do battle at the technical level with competitors. Afterward they supported the client, sorting through complex issues of systems and application programming. It was serious, high stakes stuff. There were no dull people in this arena.

Darcy came from a family of the sweetest people on earth. They were the same every day of the week as they were in Sunday school. They were the gosh-golly type of folks, with a few shucks and gee-whizzes tossed in. I got to know the family in my pre-management days, before I started coming up through the ranks while moving around the country.

When I came back to Seattle, I was in middle management. Darcy, like a lot of women, was tied to a given geography because of her husband's job as a professor. If you couldn't move, you didn't get promoted at IBM, since almost every job required a move to staff and then back to the field somewhere else. The company did not want you managing your former peers and buddies. So lots of great women, deferring to their husbands' careers, stayed and progressed only within their existing discipline, e.g. Systems Engineer to Advisory Systems Engineer, and on up the Systems Engineering career path.

I would later capitalize on the fact that IBM hadn't promoted people who wouldn't move. The fact that someone couldn't move, didn't make them any less capable, inherently. Since this usually happened with women, I developed a theory that if I could somehow promote these people past staff positions and right into field management from a non-management job, then I was picking up hidden talent. Some of the women with whom I did such "battlefield" promotions could have risen as high as they wanted to in the company. Instead, they were stuck in Seattle. In my latter days with IBM, most of my managers were women. I knew a good deal when I saw one (or several). I usually had an extremely loyal management force.

So, after our family had moved back from Connecticut where we lived during my stint at headquarters, Darcy called to ask me for some career advice. She saw what I was doing and she wanted to talk about where she should go next. I readily agreed to a meeting, not really knowing why she wanted to talk. I just knew I liked Darcy and I wanted to catch up. In addition to being perpetually happy and upbeat, she was also one of the smartest people in the Seattle office. Everybody in her family was smart and multi-talented. Her sister was a doctor and a medical school professor. Her dad, a truly humble man, was a very successful business leader in Seattle. This was not your average family.

After we finished catching up on the personal side, she told me she was there to talk to me about her career and where she should go next. This is normally done by a person's manager and since Darcy didn't report directly to me, I was not in a position to get too specific in my advice.

Like many intelligent and capable people, she was considering management as a possible option and my proclivity toward promoting women or sponsoring them for promotion had been detected by her. Her other route would be to specialize in a particular area and advance in grade as one of the Seattle technical heavyweights. We both knew that with her intellect, she surely could become one. She went over the pros and cons of each option as I listened.

One of the things I do before asking people where they would like to take their career is ask them where they would like to take their lives. Usually, when I am having that kind of conversation, discussions of money and power come up. The standard phrases are: "I would like to have enough money so that I am free to do what I want"; and "I would like to have enough authority so that I can have an influence over a meaningful portion of the company."

To the first statement regarding money, I give them my wisdom, supplemented by that of Ben Franklin's: "The amount of money a man wants is always one dollar more than he currently has." This sets the stage for the discussion of power and authority. I use my desk as a fulcrum for my clever point, since IBM was so punctilious on office size and desk size that each level in the organization had a maximum desk size.

"Okay, my desktop is 4 by 6; so it's 24 square feet. I want a bigger desk. You know what I will do when I get a desk that is 4.5 by 6.5 feet?" I ask. "I will rest my elbows on it, and dream about a 5 by 7 desk. It never ends."

The truth of the matter on the subject of wealth is that there are only two ways to become rich: accumulate more or want less. I believe the latter is highly underrated when you are young but as you reach the far side of middle age, you realize how much further ahead you would be, had you chosen the road less traveled. I drive a 12 year-old mini-van. A friend of mine in that period of time has bought and sold two Mercedes and a Jaguar. He just sold the Jaguar and is looking around for another one while driving his wife's car. He got creamed on the Jaguar's resale. I am now one green mini-van and about $150,000 ahead of him.

Let's put wealth and power aside. They are both collateral elements. You find the right amount where the rainbow ends.

Sooner or later it comes down to a combination of three things people consider for themselves and their family: where they would like to live, the types of material goods they feel will satisfy them, including a house, and finally, how much they would need to live on in order to have some degree of freedom. Darcy was one of the few people who actually knew the answers to all three. Eventually, she wanted to live in Seattle; the house they had was big enough for raising the three kids they hoped to have; and money was not a big thing. Based on her extended family's simple lifestyle, I believed she had it figured out.

She then verbally wandered around discussing how she saw getting there and how she really had to choose between a technical and a managerial pathway. I mostly listened for almost 20 minutes before she finally asked, "Okay, with all that said, what do you think makes sense?"

I was still hearing the echoes of her energetic description about how she saw her ideal life unfolding. Then I asked myself, what couple, married only a few years, decides to buy a house big enough to raise several kids? I barely heard her question as she finished her career option analysis. I was looking out the window, when I heard her repeat the question. "So, what do you think I should do? I mean if you were me, would you..."

"I think I would quit my job."

"What?"

"I think I would quit my job if I could afford to."

"I wasn't expecting that answer, Charles," she said, smiling pleasantly, with a look of curiosity.

"You want to know where that one came from?"

"Well, I hope it wasn't based on..."

"Darcy, it came from a scene that just flashed in my mind." I sat in brief reverie before continuing. "I had just started here at IBM and Kristy was working as a paralegal downtown. Each morning, I would drop off Lexie, my 5 year old daughter, at kindergarten daycare. And then right next door on the toddlers' side, I would carry in Mason who was about 15 months old but had been walking since the unbelievably early age of 8 months. Kristy had stayed home from work for the first year because the daycare center wouldn't take an infant. She loved her time home being a mom.

"The scene I remember was handing Mason to one of the women who thought my little redheaded boy was just about the cutest thing she had ever seen. Then, as I was getting into my car, I heard hands slapping at the big window of the daycare center. It was Mason, red faced, crying his lungs out. Each time he would slap the window he would scream "Daddy!" at the top of his voice. He was terrified that I was leaving him. I came back into the daycare, picked him up and cuddled him until he calmed down. I then subtly walked back over to the lady who had been holding him and said, 'I'm not sure what prompted that.'

"She apologized and said, 'I'm very sorry. That only happens when I put him down before your car leaves. If I hold him long enough, he settles down.' I asked how long this had been going on and she said that he had been doing that on and off ever since we brought him there, three months earlier. 'Normally, you're in your car by then and you can't hear him,' she added.

"I drove away in tears. That wasn't the last time I would show up to work with red eyes. Fortunately, I got promoted soon thereafter. When we moved, Kristy never took another job outside the home."

Darcy's eyes had puddled up as I described the scene of Mason slapping his little hands on the window for his daddy to come back.

"Look at you, Darcy. Look at your eyes." I handed her a Kleenex. "And this isn't even your kid. What are you going to do when it's your little red-haired boy? I know we working folk all go through that, but given the choice, knowing what Kristy and I now know about the issues of getting ourselves 'set in life,' we would never have had Kristy go to work after Mason was born.

"So the big question is...?" I sang slowly, waiting for her to fill in the blank.

"What am I going to do when my child slaps the window?" she said to herself quietly.

"You answer that and then I'll be glad to offer advice, one way or the other."

We sat there in silence for a bit before she thanked me and left without another word.

Shortly afterward, she quit.

I didn't hear from Darcy for almost 12 years. Just after I came back from living in the slums of Bombay, I started talking to her sister about a potential medical project in Africa. When we were finished, she said, "Do you have an extra minute? There's someone here who wants to talk to you."

When Darcy got on the phone, we caught up quickly. And then she thanked me for instigating what turned out to be exactly the right "career" solution.

"It wasn't what I was coming over for that day," she said, laughing. "But I'm really glad I came and talked to you."

Darcy was different. I knew it and she knew it. She had always been kind of an anomaly at IBM. She rarely dressed fashionably and her shoes were what my mom used to call "sturdy girl shoes." She had kind of a silly laugh and unlike a lot of people, she never, ever said harsh or critical things. That's how I remember Darcy. She was a civilian more than an IBMer. She was a mom. She is a mom.

Even so, telling a woman these days that she ought to go home and be a mom is legally very dangerous. It's hard to get around the obvious sexism charge. But Darcy was a friend and I wanted her to have my true opinion. If she had said she wanted to consider quitting but would also like to talk job options, I would have given thoughtful and pointed career advice.

It's been over twenty years since that morning at the daycare center with Mason. If I close my eyes, I can still hear the slap of little chubby hands against the window. It may or may not have been the best career advice I could give Darcy, but I know it was the purest counsel I had in my heart.

Darcy

Stephanie

So, a guy is pushing his cart through the grocery store. In less than twelve minutes, the football game starts. He leaves one aisle, quickly rounds the corner and starts to head down another where he almost collides with a woman who is making her way to the end of the same aisle. They both screech to a halt, whereupon he says, "Excuse me," and the woman says, "Sorry!"

Sorry? Sorry for what? For being in the way of some maniac trying to buy Cheetos for the playoffs?

Once you notice it in a place like the grocery store, it jumps out at you everywhere. I saw it all the time at work. Yes, she's being polite but I think it goes deeper than that. I think it has to do with a desire to get along. It has to do with two things: Women are safe to blame because they probably won't get physically confrontational if you push it; and women just want things to be pleasant so they say "sorry" and move on.

Often, when a husband can't find something like his keys or his wallet, he gets a little irritated with his wife. She then tries to keep the situation under control by stopping what she's doing and looking for them. He's frustrated and somehow feels she's possibly to blame – maybe she moved the lost object. I want to remind you, these are *his* keys. If it were something like the TV remote, it would definitely be her fault. It could be in his shirt pocket and he would still be bugged with her.

"Why didn't you tell me it was in my shirt pocket? It was right in plain sight! Doggone it; now I've missed the kickoff to the Notre Dame game."

"Sorry."

A lot of men do some rotten things and not only will they not apologize, they won't even acknowledge that something bad happened or that someone got hurt. On the other hand, the type of women who apologize a lot, not only confess to less than rotten things, they have a unique technique I call pre-confessing. They let you know ahead of time that *they* are sorry that *you* are going to be sorry for their upcoming, potentially sorry per-formance for which they were sorrily under-qualified to have even attempted. Part of the reason for this is they want to hear some indication that it will be okay, even if something goes wrong later on.

Such women will thoughtfully buy you a little present and when they are giving it to you will say, "It's not much." And as you open it they will say, "You're probably not going to like it." And when you pull it out of the box they'll say, "You can take it back if it's not something you want."

For these women in particular, when they do make a mistake and especially when someone gets hurt as a result, the toll it takes on them is substantial. They are awash in guilt and they are pursuing expiation anywhere they can offer something, anything to atone for their guilt. Once they do, they reject its efficacy because they still feel guilty.

Stephanie was one such woman. She felt that her failure on a major proposal had gotten her boss taken out of his job. She had in fact screwed up on the proposal. And her boss had gotten demoted. There was a link but not necessarily a direct link. It wasn't like she had snuck out in the middle of the night and delivered the proposal to a guy named Willie. Everybody had reviewed it. It was for a ten million dollar mainframe computer.

She had come up with a counter to the competitor's proposal, who was claiming that IBM was about to come out with a new line of computers. The competitor was offering a greatly discounted used computer as an interim measure for the first year, allowing the client to wait and see. IBM as a company did not sell used computers. We were therefore at a huge price disadvantage for the first year if the customer bought into the notion that a new product line was imminent.

Stephanie showed how they could lease our computer for a year and then convert the lease to a purchase if we didn't announce something in a year. We were forbidden by a Federal consent decree to talk about future announcements, known or potential. It was deemed unfair because we were such a huge player in the marketplace we could possibly keep a competitor from selling new equipment just by hinting that our next product was coming soon and it would leapfrog everything out there. Here, however the rumor tactic was being used against us.

Her analysis showed that at the end of the year, if the new product came out, they could cancel the lease, treat it as an operating expense for favorable tax treatment, and avoid maintenance fees. They could then buy the new machine which they could write off rapidly for a huge tax benefit under the ACRS tax plan. This was the more expensive outcome. If a new product didn't come out, they could purchase the new model machine they were leasing and write it off. The difference was now narrow enough for both options that the team knew they could justify to the client the benefits of staying with IBM.

Another thing IBM was forbidden to do for its own ethical reasons was to look at a competitor's proposal. They generally knew what was on the table but they couldn't look at the proposal itself. This was not a practice adhered to by some of our competitors.

IBM's proposal "fell" into the hands of our competitor who then turned it over to his own financial people. Just prior to the decision deadline, they came back and showed that the IBM proposal was based on a depreciation rate that only applied to new machines. Once it had been leased, it could not qualify for such rapid depreciation; hence the lease-to-purchase plan was much more expensive on a monthly basis than we had presented it to be. In addition, our credibility suffered. We lost.

Throughout the proposal process, the team had come to me to check the limits on behavior under the legal consent decree and the internal code of ethics. I was the "judge" for the Northeast – New York, Boston and Philadelphia. I worked with a team of seven great lawyers. We had to watch these things very closely to avoid lawsuits and Justice Department action.

In the course of the battle, I got to know Stephanie pretty well. She knew that I was formerly the large systems specialist on the West Coast. We talked strategy but almost all of our conversations ended up being about personal issues she was struggling with on just about every front. She was really dealing with some unpleasant issues at work and at home. We would often talk for an hour or more in my midtown Manhattan office.

Less than a month after the loss to the competitor, her boss was demoted to a Senior Marketing Representative position in another branch. It was announced as a lifestyle move since the branch was closer to his home. But everyone knew what had happened.

Stephanie felt awful. I explained that it was her boss's job to either catch that stuff himself or to get it in the hands of the financial guys, who could go over it and find mistakes or make the proposal even better, if he wasn't sure. He owned the loss, even though it had been her error. This had been her first large systems battle and she felt devastated.

I sat for about half an hour listening to all her other screw-ups she felt had hurt other people or were just really bad, even if there were no casualties. She was living with a mountain of emotional debt, with no plans to get out from under it. I quit trying to swat each issue. I just listened and sympathized. Then we went to the conference room where I drew a diagram on the whiteboard. I had done this before with a perpetually guilty male friend. He and I had actually developed it together.

It showed a ball dropping onto the top of a triangle with a slightly rounded peak. The triangle was labeled "remorse." To the left of the triangle was a little box labeled "regret;" on the right was a box labeled "guilt." I explained that each time she did something that she felt bad about, it landed on top of the remorse triangle. We all feel remorse immediately after messing up, especially if it causes harm to another person. But, sooner or later, that ball is going to roll one way or the other. Which way it rolled was up to her. I asked her which way she thinks she lets the ball roll. She knew the answer.

"I let it roll right into the 'guilt' box."

"Yes, you do. But the bad news is that the guilt box has a hole in the bottom." I then drew a line from the bottom of the guilt box onto a set of stairs and I labeled each step. I explained as I drew: "You see, we humans don't just let someone be guilty, we must *pronounce* them guilty (the first step). We then want justice. So if someone is guilty, they need to be *sentenced*. Next, they need to be *punished*. And that's where the problem is with people who constantly let the ball roll into the guilt box. They don't really have an effective way of punishing themselves and then moving on. It's never visible or tangible enough. So they accumulate guilt and carry it around with them, hunched over, spiritually panting. They become emotional cripples."

It's not just Stephanie that has to deal with which way the ball rolls, we all do. We need to repair any damage done and console people appropriately. And then we have to move on. We have got to let that ball roll into the regret box, where it will shrink with time, making room for the inevitable cascade of other little regrets that come rolling our way throughout our very imperfect lives.

Mostly we just have to get over it. We always think that people are focused on us and thinking about us and all our foibles. But the truth is most people are dealing with their own stuff. When you get off the morning elevator ride, they aren't waiting for the door to close so they can talk about how poorly you dress. They're thinking about how they're going to get through another day.

Guy de Maupassant once wrote a short story about a man and a woman who were going to a society function a bit above their station in life. The wife wanted to look nice so she borrowed a beautiful diamond necklace from a wealthy woman she knew. Then she lost it. The husband and wife spent the next several years working hard while scrimping and saving to be able to buy a necklace to replace the one they had lost. When they presented it to the wealthy woman, they had to remind her of the loss. The wealthy woman finally remembered and then said, "Oh, those were just glass, they weren't real diamonds."

We all ought to make sure we have a real problem that really is affecting everyone else before we worry and fuss and feel bad about what everyone else might be feeling and thinking.

This means you follow the healthy pattern of screwing up, feeling remorse, taking immediate measures to ameliorate, then moving on, i.e. get over it. When you act guilty, people think you *are* guilty. When you act flippant, people think you're a jerk. Somewhere in between is both social acceptability and sanity. Somewhere between the jerk who doesn't care if he hurts people and the woman who apologizes when her husband loses his car keys is where we all ought to live.

So I suggested to Stephanie that she spend the night thinking about how she'll feel six months from now and why she can't just feel like that sooner – like this week. "And then feel free to come back and see me," I said somewhat casually. She stood to leave. As she headed toward the door, I said with a smile, "What I will do for you tomorrow will be a huge favor. I will introduce you to my famous three-word counseling program."

"What's that?"

"You don't want me to spoil the surprise do you?"

"If it's only three words, why don't you introduce me to it now?"

"Because you have to be ready for it. That's why I wanted you to spend..."

"I'm ready."

"Okay here it is..." I took a deep breath. "Get over it."

She was not ready for that. I had seemed like such a nice guy up to that point.

She recovered a bit and asked, "Is that the way you talk to guys, when they're struggling with something like this?"

"Not always. With guys I sometimes add two more words and one of them isn't very nice."

She thought about it for a second and smiled. "Does one of them begin with the letter...?"

"Yes, it does."

"That's fair – even preferred."

"Stephanie, let me tell you what you're failing to appreciate here. This is great stuff! You are in the process of developing war stories for about two years from now when everyone is sitting around having a beer. If you don't have some degree of screwing up in your war stories, then it's just bragging. War stories are about when you took on something, made some assumptions and then got your butt kicked. If they are just stories where you lined up your target, fought courageously without a misstep and then won the day, we don't call them war stories. You know what we call them?"

"Bragging?"

"I suppose that's one word for it. Guys call it bull...stuff.[4] Winning a fight - beating up some guy you could take down easily - is not a story. Getting your butt kicked and showing up the next day carrying a two-by-four with a nail in it and making things even is a war story. What you just went through is the basis for a war story. Now get over it and go find a two-by-four."

To her credit, Stephanie sucked it up. On the outside anyway, she appeared to move on. That's a good start because something on the inside of her was telling life to go find its own damn car keys.

---

[4] Mixed company, even if there are only two of us.

Sidebar: The 'Splain-or-'Splode Instinct

One thing I emphasize in my book *A Guide to Managing Earthlings* Is to avoid asking questions that begin with "Why?" This is because I don't think it's right for any adult to have to explain himself or herself to another adult, even if they are talking to the CEO. It's undignified and humiliating.

All too often, women will explain themselves without being asked to do so. It seems to them if they aren't permitted the opportunity to explain what they have just done, they will explode. For that reason I call it the "'Splain or 'Splode" instinct.

If some guy asks me to explain myself, I'll make some suggestions as to how he can spend his time - since he won't be spending it listening to me explain *anything*. The suggestion I make is rarely carried out because it would require an amazing degree of physical flexibility.

I don't mind hearing what happened. And I often don't mind hearing the logic that led to a particular action. I just don't want to hear the psychology and concomitant mea culpa that goes along with someone screwing up. I don't want to put someone in that position. It's not nice and it violates the Golden Rule.

Rarely should you ever volunteer to explain or justify yourself. It usually isn't necessary. What happened has happened. Let's figure out what we need to do next. If someone persists in demanding an explanation, tell *him* to get over it.

In preparing women for management, I really work on this. I do it for them and I do it for the people who will work for them. Most get better at it. They overcome the instinct to constantly justify their existence. And afterward, they have never exploded.

I know. I checked all the walls.

Elizabeth

Like many working moms in their late thirties and forties, Elizabeth felt she did not have enough time to deal with her teenage daughter. From the sound of it, her daughter would have required *two* stay-at-home mothers and a Doberman pinscher.

"You're scaring me Elizabeth. I'm going to have bad dreams."

"I'm already not sleeping," she conceded. "It's some new awful surprise almost every week."

"Where's your husband on all this?"

"He doesn't really get involved. He was one of three boys. He now has two daughters and no boys. He kind of feels that the ball is entirely in my court, as determined by fate and genetics."

"How do you feel about that?"

"Like I'm on a life raft, out in the middle of the ocean — paddling all by myself."

"That sounds like task number one, Elizabeth. Mandy can't be getting mixed signals from the two of you."

"Oh, he doesn't contradict anything I say."

"Wait a second. You have one parent frantically trying to rein in your daughter and the other one is watching TV. One of them is acting like it's not all that bad. The signal is therefore that *you* are overreacting. Has he ever been close to her?"

"Not really."

"I don't want to play like some pop psychologist but do you think she's trying to get him to pay attention?"

"I think we are way beyond that. She's into her own thing and she really pays no attention to what is going on at home."

"Still, you can't fight this alone. She and her friends stole a car, she got into a fight and she comes home from school before noon many days. You've gotta get your husband involved."

"I'll talk to him tonight."

I stood and walked toward the door. Elizabeth started to stand and I said, "If you want, you can use my office so you have some privacy. I would call him right now and ask him to meet you at home. Sound serious. This isn't a nightly catch-up item."

When I got on the elevator to go outside, all I could think of was how fortunate I was that Kristy was handling the home front – that she was there every day. She was a sweet loving mom but when it came to drawing the line, she was not trying to win a popularity contest. She did better at that balance than I did. Elizabeth was playing both mom and dad. I had seen this before.

A month later, she was back in my office asking for personal time off. Mandy had run away to Los Angeles.

"I'm really sorry, Elizabeth. This isn't how you saw it when you were a schoolgirl, thinking about how it was going to be to have kids, is it?"

"Two years ago, when she was thirteen, I thought I was going to be one of the lucky parents who was going to get through the teen years with my daughter as a best friend. Now I can't even remember what that little girl looked like." She began to cry quietly, hands folded politely in her lap, shoulders shaking ever so slightly. Then, through tears, almost yelling, she talked about her disappointment that she would never achieve the sense of fulfillment that motherhood was meant to be. It would always be out of reach. I didn't respond, knowing there was more to come.

"I thought this was going to be so much better than it is," she cried.

All I could do was console her. I had no idea which way this would turn. Her husband had gotten more involved but only to threaten Mandy if she didn't shape up. It's hard to say if that triggered her running away. But she was gone and now Elizabeth had to fly to L.A. and try to get her back. She was away almost three weeks but she was able to persuade her to come home.

When she came to my office to thank me for the time off, I knew she wanted to talk about it, so I asked her how it had gone. My respect for Elizabeth was already high but now I admired her more than ever. What a trooper.

She felt better just talking about it, knowing that another human being knew her story and what she had gone through. Her husband had not gone with her.

When it was clear that she had talked it through sufficiently, I came back to something she had said in the conversation we had had just before she left for Los Angeles.

"Elizabeth, you said that you thought motherhood was supposed to be fulfilling."

"I'm long over that now."

"But do you still believe it, even though it hasn't happened for you?"

"Yes. I suppose that's the common wisdom."

"Whose wisdom? Because it doesn't sound very wise to me. In fact, it sounds like a setup."

"Are you saying, Charles, that you have never heard some-one say motherhood or parenthood was supposed to be fulfilling?"

"No. Not at all. I'm saying I've heard it too much. It isn't true and it makes you feel like you're missing out on some fundamental essence of being. Is that really what you think the purpose of having kids is – to fulfill *you*?"

"Well, if it was, it didn't work."

"But it wasn't. It was to bring another life into the world, have a family, and do the very best you could in order to send her into adulthood with a shot at a good life. I have never seen anyone try so hard and do pretty much all the right things to make that happen. You have fulfilled your mission. It would be nice if it had been a fulfilling experience all along but that isn't the plan. Go to any mom who has done what you consider to be a good job of raising her daughter and ask her how she feels when her daughter leaves for college or gets married. *That's* the point where they feel 'fulfilled.' Along the way, they sometimes feel fulfilled but much of the time they feel frustrated, overworked, and anxious. You know what other feeling I detect once the daughter has been gone for a bit, whether they actually say it or not?"

"What?"

"Relief. They are relieved. They feel like a 16 ton weight has been taken off their shoulders. Tell me one thing in life, one physical thing that can become both fulfilled and relieved at the same moment. By definition aren't those two processes about as opposite as can be?"

"So I'm not supposed to be happy?"

"I didn't say that. Be happy when happy stuff happens but not for generally experiencing motherhood during the teen years. I can tell you that there have been a lot of things I have tried to do and failed at. For almost all of them, I have given it my best. I didn't always like the outcome but I look back now and I feel really good that I gave it my best.

"Look at what you just did. You went down and lived in a crummy little motel in a not-so-nice part of L.A. and fought for over two weeks to get your daughter to come home. Elizabeth, you are without a doubt, one of the best, most courageous moms I have ever known. Often, the closest you come to fulfillment in parenthood is having as few regrets as possible. Regrets almost always come only as a result of _not_ doing something. You've done everything you could. You fulfilled your role. *That's* fulfilling. Keep at it and see how she turns out. You're giving her the best chance possible. Nobody else could have done more."

Let me give you a rule I hope you remember and pass on to your grandkids:

Your effectiveness as a parent is determined not just by all the guidance, correction, and the things you give them. In the long run, it is determined as greatly by what you are.

And you are an honorable and responsible person.

Mothers who think motherhood is supposed to be greatly fulfilling are in fact setting themselves up. They usually end up feeling a bit cheated by life. If you add a career to the mix, they then feel they are to blame for their child's less than perfect behavior and therefore, they have cheated themselves out of being fulfilled.

I'm not sure that Elizabeth felt any better when she left my office that day. I think she did but it's hard to tell in the hurricane of emotions she was dealing with. She took some more time off. When she came back, she seemed to be in good spirits most of the time, as far as anyone could judge. Elizabeth didn't believe in bleeding all over everyone when she had problems. She was very professional. Very brave.

I left the company less than a year later. That was a long time ago. Elizabeth's daughter is now approaching thirty years old, probably with a child of her own. She'll undoubtedly ask a whole lot of "why me" questions herself, someday. And she'll probably think that the pain of motherhood has reached an historic paroxysm with regards to what she's going through.

Exactly the way Eve felt.

There is really only one source of wisdom that I know of on this subject that is useful to parents of difficult children. It comes from the Book of Proverbs and it applies to all children:

> *Train a child in the way he should go,*
> *and when he is old, he will not turn from it.*

If you love your kids unreservedly, despite how they act at times, they will eventually appreciate it and you will likely have your family together for the next 50 years. Sometimes that love comes in the form of very tough discipline and sometimes it comes in getting them their first car. But love is always seen as being something you do in the best interest of the child. They too will see it and appreciate it at some point, even if it's in the rearview mirror of their own parenthood.

Daniele

What follows is a condensed, tidy version of a fairly long conversation. I went back and forth a lot in the discussion I had with Daniele because I wanted to help with what I thought was a familiar issue. But something kept gnawing at me, saying that the problem was not what it seemed. It was messy but we got there. What you're about to read is the movie version. Life is never quite this clearly played out.

At about the same time Elizabeth was having problems with Mandy, a secretary in another office, Daniele, was struggling with issues involving her daughter. The two had talked and Daniele approached me tentatively, to see if I would also talk to her about her daughter. Elizabeth was a manager who reported to me and Daniele was an administrator in another organization. It was — and is — interesting to me how women network.

An admirable thing about them is their egalitarianism. Men tend to associate only with other men at their level in the organizational or social hierarchy. Women however, will all go to lunch and the group will consist of an executive, a saleswoman, and an administrator. They are usually more interested in spending time with women their own age or at their own spot in life, rather than women close to them in "caste."

Daniele claimed that her daughter Katie was not fulfilling her responsibilities. She was starting to "wander." This was a term I heard a lot but which I never used. When a kid refuses to act right or starts to do awful things, it's rarely a case of wandering. Either they sit on their butts with their arms folded or they make a beeline to the dark side. They know what they want and what they don't want. It's true that what they want may change mercurially but when it does, they are on it hard and heavy. Even if they did decide to wander, they would research wandering on the Internet and then wander with a passion.

As always, I asked where the father was on all this. Was he helping? Was he supporting Daniele? Did he care?

"My husband died almost a year ago," she explained. The hurt she felt was still clearly present.

"You don't seem old enough to be a...a..."

"Widow?" she offered, to relieve me of having to use the word. She smiled slightly. "I suppose 'Daniele-the-widow' kinda sounds like 'Agnes-the-schoolmarm' or maybe 'Aunt Hortense-the-spinster', doesn't it?"

I liked this woman right off. She was crisp and engaging, with a wonderful sense of humor. When she described some of the recent antics of her daughter, she always seemed to put a comic spin on them somewhere in the story, despite the fact that they looked to portend bigger problems.

"You still don't seem old enough to be a widow. I'm sure you hear that a lot." It wasn't her age that was nagging at me.

"Losing Steve was very painful. He was young and full of energy one day and then too weak to walk the next. Something went wrong with his heart and they just couldn't get it figured out in time to deal with it."

"I'm really sorry. Was Katie close to him?"

"I think he tried harder than she did. Like I said, he was healthy right up to the end; but he was unemployed the last three months he was alive and he always waited for her to get home, so he could talk to her or help her with her homework. She just wanted to talk on the phone or watch TV."

"Did it bother her that he was unemployed?"

"Only in the sense that we were really starting to feel the pinch, financially. Steve felt terrible about this and I think he was trying to make up for it by being a good dad when he couldn't be a good provider. Katie wanted to have the things her friends had and he had to say 'No' over and over. Now I'm doing it."

"What kind of things did you say no to and how did she react to being told she couldn't have something?"

"Oh, the typical stuff. She wanted a coat exactly like everyone else was wearing, shoes like all her friends, the same purse. I felt like I was buying her a uniform or something for some team or special group. She instantly wanted what everyone else wanted just because they wanted it. I mean, where does it end?"

"Did she ever..."

"And what do you do?" she cut me off. "When you just don't have the money, what do you do? What was Steve supposed to do, run up a charge card balance that we couldn't pay off?" She looked at me in a matter-of-fact way. "Financially, there was really no way to close the equation. She needed to..."

I held up my hand for her to wait a bit. I spun around to the side in my chair and looked at the floor. Then I got up and went to the window. "This is really bothering me, Daniele."

She wasn't ready for this. "What?" she said with concern. "Am I ..."

"You're being too brave. You're coming in here and clinically describing something as though you're an observer. But you're not. If I lost Kristy or if Kristy lost me, there would be massive trauma for years. We are now one person. We've been one person almost from the start. The two became one right away. I listen to you - you're funny and alert. You describe your husband as full of energy. I'll bet he also had a great sense of humor.

"Sometimes, too great," she smiled, suppressing a grin, as she reflected on some moment in the past.

"What kind of music did you and Steve like?"

"What?" She waited for me to clarify. I didn't say anything. This was a technique used on me once when a sleep psychiatrist was trying to get past my defenses and understand the past. When you think about songs, it's hard not to engage the right side of the brain. Enter: the human element. I told her I was just curious and that it could help us both a bit in getting oriented.

She waited a little longer and then thought more about my question. "We were children of the seventies. He liked Kansas, and Electric Light Orchestra and Boston – you know, *More Than a Feeling*. He also liked..."

"I asked what kind of music you and Steve liked – both of you, together."

"I liked what he liked."

"Even if you didn't like it before he liked it?"

"Why are we talking about music?"

"We're talking about you – you the observer. People who have been hit with personal tragedy, especially the loss of a husband or wife, go one of two routes. Either everything is about them or everything is going on outside of them. For the latter, life is in the other room, waiting. Whenever I see someone full of life somehow shrug off the unshruggable, I know there is some kind of mechanism being used to keep the pain tolerable and to keep life manageable. Katie has popped up as an element you can't manage and she threatens to disrupt your whole inner ecosystem which is still pretty fragile."

"Charles, it's really not me. She has become almost purely materialistic," she insisted, sounding just a little frustrated.

"Compared to whom?"

This stopped her. She tried to explain that materialism is like art: you know it when you see it. She said. "When you see someone focused on *things* to the extent she is, you know that person is caught up in a materialistic..."

"Because she wants what the other kids want? That's what you said. She just wanted what everyone else wanted. Kinda sounds normal to me, Daniele."

"That's not how I see it."

"The question is, where do you see it from?"

"I don't get what you're saying."

"Since Steve died have you come to see how precious life is? How important people are? How important it is to spend time with people you love? Haven't a million thoughts like that ripped through your mind?"

"Yes."

"Daniele, this is from another seventies song – '*You don't know what you've got 'til it's gone*.' You now view life from the standpoint of someone who realizes that having lots of stuff doesn't mean anything." I sat back down and waited for a response. She was still processing this and to an extent, resisting it. I continued. "Every once in a while I think about the idea of losing Kristy. When I do, I don't think to myself, 'Boy, I wish we had more stuff.' But you don't have to think 'what if'; sadly, you're already there."

Daniele

"There's probably some truth in that. But I think I'm moving on with my life."

"Time heals."

"But don't you think my daughter is trying to find comfort in stuff, when she should be...?"

"That's exactly what I think. And unless she's just going crazy buying twenty pairs of shoes she never wears, then I would simply try to work out something with her."

"I could explain where I am financially and tell her how much I have that's discretionary."

"That's not a bad start. Then if she wants more stuff or nicer stuff, she can decide if she wants to work for it. Some people get pretty reasonable about that two hundred dollar sweater when they have to work a lot of hours to get it.

"In the meantime, I think you need to work on *you*. You may well be making progress but there's still an awful lot being held back and controlled. If I were you, I would go home and play some of the music you and Steve used to listen to. It'll probably hurt. But I think you need to feel bad, so you can start feeling good. Either you are a lot tougher than me, Daniele, or you haven't done the hard job of grieving."

The problem was more Daniele at that point than it was Katie. That's usually not the case.

Daniele was dealing prematurely with an issue many of us as parents have to confront. A lot of young people get toward their college years or are in their college years when they start really focusing on cars and clothes, a spacious apartment, a great entertainment system, and other things that can drain a family's bank account. That's when you need to have a fundamental

104

conversation that sets up a clear choice – a fork in the road. That was Daniele's original reason for talking to me.

I call it the "to-have-or-to-be" discussion. It's usually best received when delivered by someone other than the parent – someone the young person looks up to. After that, it's important that the parents reinforce it, subtly but persistently.

At about the time the high school years are ending and the third decade of life is just around the corner, your son or daughter has to understand that they are going to be forced to make a choice, based on money and even more so on their time. They have to choose between *having* stuff or *being* someone – to have or to be. Do you invest in your education, your calling in life, and develop your God-given gifts?" Or do you try to start living the "good life" now?

The young person needs to see that if you pursue *being*, you will eventually *have* what you want. But if you pursue *having* right now, you will very possibly never get to *be* what you could have been. The next tragedy is that you likely won't have the resources to *do* what you want to do. As we get older, we learn the real priorities are *being* and *doing*. *Having* is a distant third.

I have always had the good fortune to be curious about the road ahead. Starting in my mid-teens, I sought out people who were three to five years older than me and asked, "Looking back, what do you wish you had done differently during the last three or five years?" I learned a whole lot. It led to Kristy and me buying a house when she was 18 and I was a sophomore in college, working in a gas station.

It might be good to find some slightly older people your kids can talk to and see what they learn. You might want to avoid pairing them up with outright hedonists, but most people are pretty honest and they realize they could have been a little smarter with their most precious commodity – time.

Rachel

Rachel was a well-organized manager, very neat, and very nice to all of her people. She was tidy and structured in all respects. Consequently, she drove me nuts and all of her people were frustrated to the point of near-rebellion. Something had to be done. I had probably waited a bit too long. But I felt things were still salvageable.

My initial hesitation to intervene was because I had been giving her time to find her own managerial groove. She had made the mistake early on that I had warned her against - she tried to be popular. She tried to assure everyone that she was not a threat in any way. This is a mistake because by trying to be popular, you are placing too great an emphasis on your own behavior as a metric. You are saying to your people that your success and your authority are determined by how much they like you. And by being entirely non-threatening, she was taking away the potential that there could be consequences for her people not meeting the performance measurements she sets out for them. They've got to know that you have at least a couple of sharp teeth in your mouth. This is not a throwback to primordial, pre-anthropoid behavior. This is part of leadership.

Humans are very hard on leaders and they are murderously hard on people who are in positions of leadership who do not act like leaders. Rachel was in no way acting like a leader.

"So you're saying I'm being too nice?" she asked in disbelief.

"No. I'm saying you are being too weak. You are using niceness to discourage people from assaulting you. That means you are afraid of being confronted. This limits your leadership options to only those actions which will not incur a challenge by the people you are supposed to be leading. They detect that and they know you are not really capable of leading. People don't like being without a strong leader. They instinctively know it's dangerous."

"And my office is too clean?" she asked, going back to one of my statements from earlier in the conversation

"Yep. Have you always been so neat?"

"As long as I can remember. But I don't see what that…"

"It often means you are trying to keep at least something under control, which means you're scared. And it often means you are trying very hard to avoid criticism. You have probably always tried to avoid criticism."

"Well, who wants to be criticized?" She was starting to get a little testy. This was good.

"Nobody. I personally hate it."

"So…I guess I don't get it. You say I'm avoiding criticism and that's bad, even though you yourself avoid it."

"I never said I avoid it. I said I don't like it. There's a big difference. People who avoid criticism become paralyzed. A manager who avoids criticism can't make tough decisions or push when it's time to push."

"So what's that got to do with my office? Am I supposed to have more of a mess?"

"In your case, it would be a good idea."

"That's ridiculous," she said, raising her voice just a bit. Then she thought better of her response and covered her mouth. "I'm sorry; I didn't mean to say you're ridiculous."

"You didn't. You said my idea was ridiculous. And look at me. I'm still alive and I'm even smiling, despite what you said."

One big reason I was working closely with Rachel to get her management style in order was the fact that I wasn't always going to be her manager. I got to watch her from her early management days, so there was a history. I could see her progress. I felt she had a lot of smarts and if she could get past some of the personal style issues, she would be a good manager. But she simply had to toughen up. Those of us in middle to upper management are often not very nice people. She would not survive working for a lot of my peers. As a company, we were very humane in dealing with under-performing employees. That compassion did not extend to managers quite as often.

When I was a higher level local manager in IBM, I once had a Japanese woman work for me who had been put on special assignment. She was to help me on a small project I had undertaken. In return it was a chance for her to get more exposure to upper management, so we might be better able to determine if she was ready for management herself. It was what we called a "developmental opportunity."

She was highly intelligent. I liked that part. But she was unbelievably frightened of me to the point of having a dry, sticky mouth and gulping a lot. I was new to the area and a bit of an unknown quantity. If she started to say something and I started to say something at about the same time, she would apologize profusely. This was starting to bug me. I felt like some ogre.

But what really drove me crazy was the fact that she would bow as she entered my office. This may seem like it was just a Japanese thing, which it kind of was, but she was born in America and raised in a non-Japanese suburb. And outside my office, she was one of the gang.

I finally told her she was walking on eggshells and she needed to stop. I also told her not to bow anymore when she crossed the threshold to my office. She agreed, reluctantly.

She got a little surer of herself in conversation, but she was still pretty far off of where she would need to be if she ever had any hope of being considered for management by the people at my level. And she did something even worse...

She kept bowing when she came into my office.

I would call her on it. She would apologize and not do it for a while. But then after a couple of days, she would do a modified bow – not quite so deep. I told her no more bowing. Period.

A week later, as the deadline for my project's completion approached, she came into my office and did a bow just like the bad old days. She sat down and started to give me her status. I interrupted. "Lisa, you bowed." I held up my hand as she started to apologize. I said, "Don't worry. I've come up with a cure. You just need to go back outside and do this all over." The look on her face was one of complete shock – as in I-just-grabbed-a-fallen-power-line shock.

"Does that mean I need to...?"

"Lisa, it doesn't mean anything other than you need to leave my office. You still have to give me a status. We're running out of time. So you need to go out of my office, take a deep breath and come back in. Can you do that?"

She didn't understand but she nodded and stood up, giving me an are-you-sure look.

As she neared the door, I added, "When you come back in, you need to give me the status..." she nodded in understanding. "...and Lisa, early on, to get my attention, you need to call me a dirty name."

She opened her mouth to protest but I barked playfully, "Go on! I'm expecting a visit in the next minute or so...from you." Turning back to my computer, I started clicking away on my keyboard. Less than thirty seconds later, she tapped at my door and walked in, hesitantly, without a bow. I continued typing.

She started talking to me, clearing her throat every few seconds as she spoke. I continued typing away and every once in a while I would look over at her with a smile. At one point I held my hand to my ear and leaned a bit in her direction. I said to myself, "I thought I heard something." I shook my head and went back to typing. "I must be getting old."

She stopped talking. I waited. Finally she spoke.

"Okay, Charles..you son of a bitch, I have the..."

I instantly spun around in my chair, big smile on my face, arms wide open like the happiest guy on earth and said, "There you go! Now don't you feel better? Because I do."

This was a tough but necessary lesson for a woman raised in a Japanese household who simply was too subservient to those in positions of authority. Management is not a country club. We often talk to each other harshly. You have to be a lot tougher in a big company to move up the ladder. Lisa would have had no chance to even get to the first rung. It's bad when managers can't challenge or be challenged.

In the final months I spent at IBM, we had more or less a Board of Directors for the Northwest, led by the person who managed the entire Region. I was the executive responsible for IBM's consulting services. There were eight of us – all men - in that room about once a week. We yelled and gestured. We pounded our chests and threatened. Unfortunately, women rarely got to see that. When a woman would come into the room, we quit swearing and threatening to kill each other. We sat up straight. They thought we were polite and civilized. We were. Until she left and then it was back to Murder on the Orient Express.

Back to Rachel. It took her a long time. I never made her call me a son of a bitch. But I came close. One time when she had worked her tail off on something, I thanked her for her hard work and then I had to tell her, it was not what I wanted. It was not even close. She was solving yesterday's problems. She had to redo everything. I felt kind of bad but she hadn't listened.

She was obviously very disturbed. And I kind of took advantage of it.

"Rachel, you'd like to strangle me about now, wouldn't ya?"

"No. I just think I could maybe take the first..."

"If you think there's anything salvageable in there –anything whatsoever – you're wrong."

"But there's..."

"Throw it away and start over."

She fumed quietly.

"Admit it. You think I'm a jerk and you'd like to strangle me."

"I don't..."

"Well, *I* think I'm being a jerk. Can't you tell a jerk when you see one? This jerk just told you all your hard work was for naught. And he said it like, 'Just toss your gum wrapper in here.' Wouldn't you like to strangle me? Just say it."

She took a deep breath.

"Say it," I taunted.

She took another deep breath. "I would really, really, really like to strangle you," she said firmly and with an alarming amount of conviction.

"Until my eyes pop out of my head?"

"Until your eyes pop out of your head and hit that window," she declared, pointing intensely at the window behind her.

"Feel better?"

"Yes."

"Me too."

I won't say that was a breakthrough but it was a start.

I had to get her out of other nasty habits – or I should say she needed to get out of some nasty habits. She would never just say, "I think we need to do X." Or better yet, "We need to do X." Instead she would say in a beseeching voice, "Don't you think, maybe it would be a good idea if perhaps we did, I don't know, like X?"

A study in the 70s showed that in a conversation with a man, women will ask far more questions – mostly with the intent to be overly polite. If that's what women want to do outside of work, it's up to them. Although, having your own opinion and being able to state it freely is pretty nice. But at work, you have to be able to say, "This is what we need to do." You can't position an idea and hope the other person picks it up. You can't hope that somebody figures out what you're trying to get them to do. You can't ask if maybe, perhaps this is a good idea. You need to state it.

The other thing I had to work on was the degree to which she walked on eggshells after making a tough or unpopular decision. "Don't do that," I told her. "It cedes ownership to your boss or your critics. Own your decisions good or bad so that you also own and control the next step. If it breaks, you want to be the one who fixes it."

Don't ever walk on eggshells, even if you feel horrible about something. Do your best to fix it. Do it quietly and move on. And don't bleed all over everybody.

People also tend to walk on eggshells if they have a moody boss. Don't tiptoe around that guy, either. It feeds his moodiness. He is often just using it for power. Don't respond to it. *He's* got a problem. Not you.

Early, one Monday morning, I got a visit from one of her employees. He wanted to talk to me about a transfer.

"Have you talked to Rachel about this, Don?"

"I figured you would be the one making the decision on a transfer." Don and I went back to when I first started at IBM.

"Ultimately, yes. But you ought to let her know what you're thinking. Her recommendation would be part of my decision."

"You and I have been talking about this since long before Rachel showed up. I was really hoping not to have to start over. It's a pretty simple decision, isn't it?"

"Still, it's a matter of protocol. Can you just run it past her as both a necessary step along the way and also as a courtesy? Let her have some input. There are going to be issues of timing, backup, and other alternatives in her unit. She needs to have the opportunity to work that out with you."

"You're right. That makes sense. I'll chat with her."

"If you want to keep things moving, work through those issues *prior* to her sitting down with me because I am certainly going to ask *her* those questions."

Rachel was devastated. She covered none of the issues of timing, backup, etc. She focused almost exclusively on why he wanted a transfer. It became clear to both Don and her that the conversation was going nowhere. Her initial step in the process was to tell him she needed to think about it. What she should have done, even if she wanted to think about it, was to give him either an initial leaning or let him know that she was open to it. She did neither. She had been mostly *reacting* as soon as he told her the subject.

Her version of thinking about it was to come to my office about 8 seconds after Don left hers.

"I can't believe he wants to quit!" she said, in clear distress.

"He's not quitting. He's asking for a transfer."

"I mean quitting my unit."

"So, what's your plan?"

"I don't know."

"Well then, what's the next step?"

"He still hasn't told me why he wants to leave."

"He said nothing? I'm surprised. That doesn't sound like..."

"He said he wants to go to the Utilities and Energy unit to get some additional experience selling to another industry."

"That kinda sounds like a reason to me, Rachel"

"But he's 53. Why is he looking for a new experience? How is he going to use it?"

"I would be careful with that one."

"I know, I know. It's just that...I don't know. I'm thinking...Oh, I don't know what to think."

"You think he's leaving your party early. You just put out the brownies you baked and you see him putting on his coat."

"What?"

"You're taking it personally. You're seeing it as a rejection of *you*. It's like a mini-divorce to some people. But even if you're certain it's a slap at you, it's still a business issue and you need to handle it professionally, not personally. Just out of curiosity, what bothers you most about him asking to go to another unit?"

"I guess it's the fact that we just had a review with the team and he said nothing about this. He seemed pleasant and participative. He didn't give me any hint he wanted to leave."

"You're really making this sound like a divorce. In a way, we've talked about this before. You try to do everything you can to avoid a confrontation, because you're not sure you could handle the outcome. Now Don has gone right around the confrontation part and given you the outcome. You thought everything was under control. You had everything in order and then this." She didn't respond. She knew this was the right assessment of her reaction and her general approach to keeping the world in order. So I continued.

"Here's what I would like you to do. Come back and tell me what your plan is for handling this. And then I want you to tell me how this can be an opportunity for everybody to come out ahead – you, me, Don, your unit, everybody. Make a list of the basic things you need to discuss with Don and review it with me. Then you'll need to make your recommendation to me."

This was her first transfer. There are actually a lot of items you have to consider in the process. I know I missed a lot of things the first time I had to deal with this as a new manager.

And by the way, back then I kind of felt like that guy was leaving *my* party early. I had only been there about a month or so when the employee asked for a transfer. My first thought was, "He doesn't want to work for *ME!*" Most people feel that way. But again, women tend to take it more personally. Even when they hate the guy who's leaving, they still are more than a little bit hurt. I believe it has to do with the fact that women take most relationships more seriously than the average guy.

Rachel had a particularly tough time with all this. Part of it was her desire for order and control. A lot of women use this in hopes of protecting themselves from hurt. It rarely works. My advice when I see it is: Get things in *generally good* order and then work on the big stuff. Figure out what the one or two most important things you or your organization must accomplish in the next several months to a year, then focus entirely on that. If bad stuff happens, you can deal with it and you almost always can get all the help you need when it does.

After all, isn't it better to trust your capabilities and build a support team than it is to constantly make sure that everything is in order – especially when you know you will never get everything in order?

Over time, the most important thing I could do for Rachel was to get her to lighten up and let go. One good way to do that was to help her develop a sense of humor. It took a fair amount of excavation to mine the first few ounces of humor, but after a while she got to the point where she could trust herself to show a little wit. When I refused to take her seriously on a number of "grave and threatening" issues she brought to me, but made jokes instead, she finally got to where she could joke about it too. A little gallows humor is healthy - even if you really are about to be hanged. There was hope for Rachel.

As an aside on this subject, my business partner and I were in a filthy, illicit lawsuit brought against our startup by a billion dollar company that sued because it was getting its butt kicked by our firm. As we were in the lobby about to go into the mediation which would determine if our company would survive, our lawyer was horrified to see how we were taking it. Even *he* was nervous. Bill and I looked at each other, eyes narrowed. I slapped him on the shoulder, saying, "See you in Hell, Bill." We bumped fists and he growled, "See you in Hell."

Just like in the movies.

Which brings me to my final point:

This is all just a movie. When this battle scene ends, we're going to get up off the ground and star in another movie. So, when you brush the dust off, do it with a smile and a bit of class. Don't take it so seriously.

In other words – we all need get over it.

Ann

I hesitated to add this story but a couple of women with real wisdom encouraged me to do so. And then In writing it, I came up with some reasons of my own that I had missed seeing all these years.

I just wish I could have this story back in real time. I want to play it once again and do something that will somehow make things turn out differently. But I know that I have my limits as to what I can affect and effect in life. I did what was right, with all good intentions. But still...

In my first days at the helm of a 700-person technology company, I understood something that the owners I was taking over for did not seem to fully grasp: we were in a battle for talented people in a tight, tight resource market. The dotcom boom was at its peak, yet we had gone flat amid huge demand for our services. We needed to do a better job of finding and attracting top talent. We had gone from 15% growth to 6% growth to 0% growth. We were only able to replace as many people as we lost but we could not gain traction.

I decided to more than double the number of recruiters. We had five and we needed to get to twelve, by my projections. This was not sitting well with the former owners and most of the recruiters were pretty unhappy as well. After all, recruiters were paid a salary plus a fee for each person they hired. To them, doubling the number of recruiters translated directly to cutting their pay in half. Like many people's view of the world today, they felt the pie was as big as it was going to get. I had other plans. They were for rapid change and I would need a recruiting manager to help implement those plans.

Emily was the only one of the recruiters who had the potential for leadership. She had just turned 30 and had a little management experience. She was smart, classy, and confident. But if you are young and inexperienced and then you are asked to manage a group of your former peers, it's just too much. That's why IBM almost always made us move, take a staff job to learn more about how the business works, and then we would often move again to manage people in another location.

Sid Christenson, a former owner and president, was a strong advocate of Emily's. When he finally understood that I was going to hire a recruiting manager and grow that department over his and the other former owners' objections, he came to me and made the case for her getting the job. I listened but my mind was made up. Nothing he said helped. In fact, it moved me further to my side because she just didn't have any experience that could translate and Sid's rendition of the department's recent woes made it sound like a real mess. He asked if he could be the one that explained it to Emily because he had a history with her. I agreed but explained that she needed to hear it from me as well.

I went to an outside search firm and told them what I was looking for. Sharon, the firm's senior partner went about the job diligently and within two weeks had sourced four candidates. But they just didn't have it. Sharon explained that it was a tough market for recruiters and recruiting managers too. I understood but I said, "Come on, Sharon. There's got to be someone out there. That's where you live! You have a whole network of recruiters. Isn't there anyone else?" There was a long pause. I wasn't sure why. I wasn't trying to hurt her feelings or pressure her unduly.

"I have one other candidate but I wasn't sure she would be acceptable to you," she said dryly.

"Why not? Credentials? Attitude? Great big nose ring?" My thoughts went immediately to a man who had just been in my office wondering why he wasn't being considered for a new project manager position that had just opened up. Besides atrocious interpersonal habits, on one hand he had the letters *h-a-t-e* tattooed in a sort of Rune alphabet on each knuckle. On the other hand was *d-e-a-t-h*. Ringing his neck was another tattoo that said *it-all-ends*. All I could think was, "Who hired this guy in the first place?" The dotcom era had some very porous filters. We definitely needed to get control of our hiring process.

"Well...Charles...she's bald."

"I guess it depends on why she's bald," I responded flatly.

"She just finished chemo. She had breast cancer but it's now in remission. Her hair will eventually grow back," she quickly assured me.

"I actually am not concerned if it doesn't grow back, other than I'll bet she really wants to have a full head of hair again."

"So you would consider her?"

"Of course I would. It's a golden rule issue. How would I want to be treated in that situation?" I said with an edge of frustration.

"I just didn't think you..."

"Let me ask you this, Sharon. Would you have held her back from me if I were a woman?"

The silence answered my question.

I continued. "Look, you don't know me very well and you may have some idea as to how a man's mind works but please don't sort me into that pile so readily. I've lost a lot of friends and family members to this epidemic of breast cancer and I have had nothing to offer as I watched from the sidelines. Even the ones who survived had gone through something so rough it...it just isn't fair. Maybe she'll work out and maybe she's not the right person for the job but she at least needs to have a chance at normalcy. If there was one thing I heard from the women I knew who had breast cancer it was a desire to just have a normal life again with normal options. Let me give her that option if she's qualified."

"Okay, I'll send you her information."

"And please don't do that to me again, Sharon. I like pretty women and I think classy women who dress nicely and do their hair up every day really add to the scenery but that's not how I make hiring decisions."

"I'm sorry. I won't make that mistake again."

"Thank you."

When Ann walked into my office two days later, I was instantly struck by her energy and charm. She had a long, loosely flowing dress of blue, streaked with purple – and a floppy round cloth hat that almost matched exactly. I thought of the amount of time she must have spent picking out something, fitting it to her perfectly smooth head, and asking, "What do you think?" first to the person at the store and then probably a dozen times to her husband. "Do you think this looks okay?" she would ask him. "Are you sure this looks okay?" she would try again. "This looks silly, doesn't it?" she would test. That was his cue for the affirmative approach, which he would take in all sincerity, if he were any kind of a husband.

When husbands say, "Yes, dear" or "That looks fine" or, worst of all, "It doesn't matter," they are abdicating. Who else is a woman going to turn to when she's trying to figure all this out? In a way, I almost feel sorry for husbands who don't get into it. How often in the course of a year and therefore the course of your marriage and your life do you really get to do that kind of a thing? I say almost feel sorry because they're the same guys who will let their wives spend three hours cooking something and then don't say anything until asked; at which point they'll grunt, "It's okay."

I really hoped Ann had the right kind of husband. But it turned out she wasn't married.

Within 30 minutes I knew she was everything her resume said she was. In addition, she was smart, engaging, and articulate. She had a great sense of humor. We had a lot of laughs. I knew I was going to enjoy working with her.

The only problem was that she felt an obligation to the company she was now working for that had stood with her during her breast cancer ordeal. They knew she was looking elsewhere and the parting was going to be amicable. But she needed a two-month transition.

"That's a long time, Ann. But you're worth waiting for. Can we transition a bit on this side of things as well?"

"What do you mean?" she asked.

"Well, I've got to ramp up the number of recruiters and I think you should have a say as to whom we hire, how we segregate workload, how people get compensated, etc. Don't you think? Besides, there is a woman in the department who is future management material and I think she will do a great job as your right-hand person during the transition." I described Emily. Ann agreed. I didn't bother with the background regarding Emily having once been a candidate for Ann's job – at least in Emily and Sid's minds. Why complicate things? Ann was already dealing with a lot of moving pieces. Besides, I sensed that Ann would become more than just a recruiting manager. She had a fair amount of middle management experience in a large firm in Seattle. She would eventually be a member of the executive team I envisioned building to replace the old guard of former owners.

I set up a couple more interviews for Ann with Sid and Lloyd, the former CEO. They would soon see what I saw. In the meantime, I sat down with Sid and explained where I was in the process and I asked him how his conversation with Emily had gone. He had had two days to deliver the message. It turns out that all he told her was that I was looking at other options in addition to Emily. He couldn't look me in the eye. He knew what he had done by not telling her straight out.

"I really wanted to make sure that this Ann person was a go," he explained, recovering. "Now that she is, I need to take it up a notch and really level with Emily." I just stared.

"Sid, you had your shot. I'm not going to let this get any messier or drag on any longer. I'll explain it to her. She'll be fine. She is incredibly mature. She'll probably be disappointed but she'll be fine. Besides, under Ann's tutelage, she'll probably get the job at some point and it won't be all that long, given the rate I plan to get things going." [Note: we went from 0% growth to 74% growth that year.]

"What if she isn't fine?" he demanded. I wasn't pleased by his tone. These guys had been anything but advocates of change and their support for me had been hideous. I was making unpopular decisions, whereupon they would commiserate with the people who got their nose bent out of joint.

"I make the decision... and then I clean up the mess. That's how it works. Just the opposite of the way you guys have operated."

"What the hell does that mean!?" Once again, the gloves were off between Sid and me.

"It means you guys make a mess and then you're forced to make a decision. I like my way."

Emily was stoic in our meeting. She said she understood but it was clearly a disappointment. Evidently Sid had been telling her for some time prior to my arrival that she was in line for the job, should it ever open up. He had failed to mention that to me. It was really a shame because Emily was a great person. I would have hated to lose her by mishandling the communications the way we had.

"I think you'll find a wonderful mentor in Ann," I offered to Emily. "She is a very experienced manager. Her job is to help me build that operation, get it under control, and then help me with other areas of the business. She's going to need you and your role will gradually expand." That was as far as I wanted to go in reading from the crystal ball. More than that would not have been appropriate. It never is.

Ann and Emily met regularly. It was clear that they were becoming friends.

"You were right about Ann," Emily told me one day. I perked up. But before I could say anything she said, "And you were right about me."

"In what way?"

"I have so much to learn. I just didn't know what I didn't know."

"Are you learning lots now?"

"Tons. It's amazing."

That really made my day. Emily was truly a class act and far more mature than I had been at her age.

Now I was on to another key hire. I needed a branch manager for our Seattle operation – the company flagship operation with over 300 employees. Ann would report to whoever that executive was. I had narrowed the search to three people. All were great candidates.

In mid-December I took Ann to lunch. I wanted to see how she felt about things. I also wanted to know why she was leaving her current job. It was mostly out of curiosity but I also wanted to make sure that her new home would be what she wanted and that we didn't replicate any of the negative appurtenances of her prior office environment, if we could help it.

"I actually made up my mind to leave quite a while ago. Things were changing. A new team of managers was coming in – a younger team. They were nice enough but after a while some of us gals in our late 30s and 40s and beyond were kind of out of the loop socially. We weren't included in decisions and after a while we weren't included in regular conversation. I was lonely. I'm not good at being alone. In my first interview with you, Charles, I probably laughed more than I had in a year at my old place. It was just so good to talk to someone. And you asked me about my hat. No one ever said a word about what I wore and the fact that I was bald. It was like... I didn't exist."

"I wanted to know how your hat stayed on."

"Have you figured it out yet?"

"Nope."

"Okay. Tell me when you give up."

"I don't give up."

"I figured that out about you a long time ago, Charles."

As we rolled into January, we set a date to announce Ann to her team and the rest of the office. It would take place on a Thursday. Things were turning around at the company and we were starting to grow again but there was a very complex process of change underway and I needed help. I had a number of conversations with her every week. They were about business initially but we would always end up on about a dozen other tangents. She was a great conversationalist.

When my phone rang on Tuesday evening, I was pleased to hear Ann's voice. I had been thinking about her and how we were going to handle the announcement logistics. But her voice was flat. Something was wrong.

"Ann, what's up? You don't sound like your perky self?"

"I have some bad news."

"Oh, no," I thought. "She's changed her mind."

"I went in for my final screening at the hospital today. They found a mass."

"How big?"

"Monstrous. They don't know how they missed it."

"Ann, I'm so sorry. What a setback. What's the plan now? I'm assuming you need more time. Don't worry about..."

"There is no plan."

"What? I'm not sure what you mean."

"Charles, I'm going to die."

"No."

"Yes."

"Ann, you can't just say that! There's always..."

"I have two months at the most."

Ann

We both sat in silence. We had done that before in our conversations but always to reflect on something – some mutual discovery about the universe and all the crazy people that are in it. This time I just didn't know how to respond.

"Ann, I don't know what to say. I just... Is it okay to ask you how you're feeling? I would be numb."

She began by telling me that this was not the first time and that she was more or less a veteran of bad news. She explained that the ordeal started with a doctor telling her she had cancer when she had no reason to expect anything other than what she had always been told after a mammogram or other tests. And then it got worse and then it got better and then there were setbacks and then there was hope and finally progress.

"So, I guess I've been here before. Though, if I had to say how it's different, this is the first time when there are no more moves left on the board. But in a way, I've been here."

"So then are you telling me you're inured to it? You're really accepting what they..."

And then she made a sound that will haunt me the rest of my life. There was a catch in her voice and then a hoarse whisper. "Charles, I'm so scared."

My wrists ached. The sides of my head seared with pain. I felt this helpless floating... awful, swimming feeling as her voiceless statement echoed down a dark, dark funnel in my mind. I had never had someone tell me they were going to die before. How could I be 44 years old and not have heard those words until now?

Emily took the news quietly the next morning. She said very little and then left for the day. She had come to admire, respect, and like Ann.

A week later I brought her into my office and we talked about what she had learned in working with Ann. She saw where I was going and interrupted me. "I learned that I'm not ready, Charles. I'm just not ready. I'm not Ann or anything close to Ann."

Shortly thereafter, I made my selection for the executive to run the Seattle office – the person who would have been Ann's boss. Matthew was an experienced manager who really knew the business. We shared a lot of great stories during the interview process. I really liked the guy. He was older than me and frankly more mature. I needed some of that for all the sober decisions that were going to be made. He was a good man.

While I was talking to Matthew, Emily walked by my office. I called out to her. After introductions and a few minutes of conversation, I brought up the subject of the need for a recruiting manager. She took on a non-receptive posture.

"So, here's my issue, Emily. I need to get going in building the recruiting department. And I will need your help. In fact, I'll need you to do it for me. So, you will have to take on a bunch of work and run the department. You can have a nice new title, a bigger office, and more pay..."

She started to speak but I cut her off.

"As I was saying you can have all that... or you can stay in your office, have no title, no pay increase... but you're still going to run the department. It's your choice. Now I don't want you to feel pressured, so you don't have to answer right now. So go on back to your dinky little office and mull it over and then come back in a while and tell me what your decision is."

She started to speak but I held up my hand again. I told her I wanted her to have the time to think it over. She smiled and left. For protocol reasons this would be something for her and

Matthew to work out. As I watched her walk away, I realized this was yet one more case of a woman who knew every little thing wrong with herself and all her shortcomings, non-substantive as they were. And like so many other terrific women, I was going to have to put my foot in the small of her back and shove her into her career as a leader and manager.

She was a marvelous manager and incredibly loyal to me. After I left the company two years later, she along with 475 of the 600 people in Seattle went elsewhere. She became a vice president at a large Seattle firm. Emily was a natural executive.

Final thoughts on this chapter

I hesitated to write this chapter about Ann. Not because I avoid writing about painful things. I've done that a number of times. I think it was mostly a rest-in-peace sentiment.

When I mentioned this to a woman who herself had survived cancer, she disagreed. "Do you realize how little is ever written by the other people who are affected by breast cancer?" she explained. "It has almost always fallen on the woman herself to try to tell her story and, in doing so, reflect, as best she can, the feelings of those around her."

"But I wasn't part of some inner circle who had stood by her throughout the ordeal," I pushed back.

"You were close enough."

"How do you figure?"

"You were close enough to have seen the human being in her – the woman in her still fighting to be a woman. And you responded with the most important gift you could give her."

"What's that?"

"A shot at normalcy."

There was one other thing that came out at me as I wrote all this down. I don't know how I missed its importance previously. It was something I had mentioned before because I have told this story to a couple of people. And it's something that I hope everyone will take notice of. Recall that when I asked Ann why she was leaving her former company, she traced her thinking and then followed it to a conclusion that she was just plain lonely. She and others her age and older had become non-persons in an office they had worked in for years. Women sometimes get used to being displaced for men's attention by younger women. But to be almost entirely ignored by other women is a spiritual death sentence. I'm hoping in the Great Beyond to find out if in fact that is what led to Ann's cancer.

When a woman gets dressed, unless she's unattached and going bar-hopping on a Friday night, she's not really dressing for men. She's dressing for the approval and comments of other women. "Where did you get that? I really like the way the sleeves puff out. Are those buttons real wood? They look like real wood."

When I had asked Ann about her hat in that first interview, she first kind of checked me out to make sure I was sincere. Before long, she was taking it off, reading the label (it was raw silk and something else), tugging on the material to show that the something else gave it just enough stretchiness. She was smiling and happy just to be having a normal conversation with a normal person whom she suspected viewed her as a normal person too.

When I left that company a couple years later and started my own company, I got a call from Pat, a woman in her late 50s who worked in the accounting department. I told her I really couldn't hire her because of legal restrictions from my employment contract. She understood. And then about a month later, I got a message from my receptionist saying there was a woman in the lobby who wanted to see me. When I went out to see who it was, there was Pat. She was very nervous and it looked like she had been crying. She had just quit her job and drove over to see if I would hire her. Not a great strategy normally. Legally, I could hire her, since she was no longer an employee of my former company. Unfortunately, I didn't have a need for her. But I knew I would, so I hired her. She told me that after I left, things changed and she was isolated. "No one ever talked to me. I was lonely."

I really believe that the breast cancer epidemic has its roots in something besides diet and lifestyle. When I think back on all the women featured in this book who came to talk to me, it's clear that most of them simply had no one else they felt they could share with. That's not how it has been for women for the last 100,000 years. The problems they brought were often a bit heavier than day-to-day, chit-chat stuff. But frankly, problems, even big ones, are part of normal life. And so is talking about them.

We could all move the ball forward on the health front if we just talked to one another more, asked a few more questions, and honestly listened to hear not just the words but the music that makes each of us special – and normal.

Concluding Thoughts

I mentioned that it was my Jewish lady-friend who clued me in on the fact that I was having a lot more of the conversations you've just read about than the average manager. But it was the women I met and became friends with in Africa and India that opened my eyes to a broader picture. They made me acutely aware of the fact that women worldwide don't have it all that great. They told me their stories. I saw for myself a lot of what they were talking about. It was pretty raw and rough. I've told a few of their stories in my book *Breath of Kenya*. Someday, I'll share more of those conversations, told to me with whispered words and furtive glances.

It's certainly better here in the Western world. But I think it's still harder to be a woman than it is to be a man. I believe this will be true ten thousand years from now as well. It's not just the huge physical disparity; it's a matter of the wiring. And the less we are aware of that wiring, the more likely we all are to do things that are hurtful to women.

Being more aware that women view the world differently and therefore approach life differently, does not make me an expert. It doesn't even make me right. But it does make me try a little harder. Right or wrong, I gave the most thoughtful advice I could give to my sisters on this planet - my fellow human beings.

What I set out to do in this book was share meaningful conversations I had with many women and then add a couple thoughts to go along with the issues we discussed. Those conversations changed me. They gave me a perspective I might have missed. And for that I will always be grateful to the women who, with honesty, sincerity, and trust, came into my office.

Twenty-One Rules for Women to Live (Better) By

Start with the fundamental tenet that virtually all of your problems in life are due to choices *you* have made. The view that exogenous influences determine the course of your life is simply wrong. It is destructive. Don't adopt it. You are more capable than you think.

The fact is women often take a different route than most men to whatever the destination or immediate objective is. We all benefit from creating lots of routes. Good husbands, wives, managers, and friends will accept the slight variations in approach taken by individuals in either gender. An effective manager focuses on the objective, and not so much on how you get there.

There are some simple rules I live by that I have found useful. What follows are some of those rules plus a few additional ones that might be helpful, mostly to women. These are distilled from the issues which many women and I have thoughtfully worked through, during those most personal and special times when they came for a visit.

The Twenty One Rules

1. You're going to be okay. Really. So assume that you're going to be okay and act that way. Never worry visibly.

2. People are not thinking about you as critically as you are. Quit reading their minds. They can't even read their own minds.

3. Quit feeling like you have to explain everything. You did what you did. Move on. If the other person can't move on, that's their problem. You can sometimes explain out of courtesy or caring; but don't do it to justify yourself.

4. Quit feeling guilty. Turn temporary remorse into regret and never let it turn to guilt. You are trying to be a good person. People who try to be good people *are* good people. Therefore, you are not guilty. Move on.

5. Assume you are better than you think you are. Act that way and any gap that exists between your image and your performance will probably close up. Be persistent.

6. Get over it.

7. Say what you mean. Say it pleasantly. And say it in one step. Don't get there with little set ups and positioning moves. Have you noticed those moves never turn out as planned?

8. Be feminine. Margaret Thatcher was able to power her way through a lot of opposition – mostly made up of men – and never once lost her feminine comportment.

9.   Never get caught in the trap of believing that men and women are judged the same way. Even if laws are passed and people are executed for treating women and men differently, they always will. Adjust to it. Take advantage of it. Thrive as a result of it.

10. Quit defending yourself. Unless you're being attacked outright, say "I disagree." There, you're all done with that particular subject.

11. Remember Abraham Lincoln's favorite saying: "And this too shall pass." Think of the 5 most embarrassing things that happened last year. You can't! They all passed. This will too. Later, they will be great war stories to regale all your friends.

12. When you want to make a point, make statements, don't ask questions. Instead of saying, "Don't you think we should include X in our proposal," say "I think X needs to be in our proposal." You don't have to get some guy's approval for your thoughts and opinions. Guys don't work their way up to stating their position – real guys, anyway.

13. Quit saying awful things to yourself over and over. "I'm such an idiot." "I'm a failure." "Everybody hates me." And quit saying: always, everybody, and never.

14. Quit confessing and pre-confessing. Quit revealing your evil deeds of years gone by on the off chance that someone is going to find out about them anyway.

15. Talk about how nice it was when you went for a hike. Don't sit there waiting for your chance to talk about your blister or the rock you had in your shoe the whole way. Especially don't do this around guys. We like war stories. But unless a grizzly bear ripped off your arm, we don't want to hear about it. Anything short of that is whining.

16. Seldom use the words "should" and "should have." This is part of the self-loathing, I'm-such-a-failure syndrome. Say: I will or I won't; I did or I didn't.

17. Don't tell people everything about your private life – good or bad. Leave room for a little mystery.

18. Don't extrapolate. Just because it is worse today than yesterday, doesn't mean it's going to get totally, insolubly awful. Don't draw a line through two events on the graph and extend it downward. It always goes straight to hell. And don't say, "I can't stand it!" You're here aren't you? You obviously *can* stand it.

19. Forgive more quickly. Forgive completely. Men either work it out or they agree to remain openly hostile. Women have traditionally had fewer ways to work it out. (i.e. they won't punch each other). It's not acceptable to say women hold grudges more often and longer than men. But many people believe it. Thus forgiveness and burying the hatchet will require an overt act of peacemaking. Otherwise, it will be assumed you are holding a grudge and you can't be fully trusted. And when you bury the hatchet, don't leave the handle sticking up. Everybody knows what you're doing.

20. Don't act like a guy. Don't swear and talk dirty, even if the guys are doing so. Nobody will say anything, but the guys who are worth a darn do not think highly of women who let their morality and civility slip, even a little. And don't expect men to act or think like a woman, even if it would be the right thing to do in a particular situation. We're neither that flexible nor that noble. Don't you have enough trouble trying to get men to act like *men*?

21. Never forget that women are the keepers of the culture. When women no longer do their job of keeping society decent - whether out of a lack of diligence, the allure of the material world, or due to oppression - the culture and the country will fall apart.

The difference in approach between men and women is a problem only when either gender takes those differences too far. And while it can sometimes work against women, the fact that there is a difference is not necessarily based on a bad thing.

Looking at the way women approach an issue more gently, ask more questions, and even apologize more readily, it seems to me to be part of maintaining civility and therefore the culture. I hope for everyone's sake, the differences never fully go away.

Bonus Rule # 22

Men do not grow up.

Do not hope that someday your husband will be fully mature. Men do not reach maturity until at least 50 years after they die and someone writes about them, leaving out all the immature things they did right up to the end of their life.

Corollary to Rule 22: If by chance you have a husband that you feel is fully mature, he is probably a pretty dull guy.

If your husband is still kind of full of himself, still trying to attempt stupid things to prove his manhood, still embarrassing you at the grocery store, then you're in good shape.

At work, we appear to be mature when you're around. But get us in a room by ourselves for a while and you'll realize it hasn't been all that long since we graduated from Junior High. Once we're back in with the rest of the people, we executives have that look on our face like we're inspecting the whole planet to see if it's suitable for carbon-based life.

"Are we still 93 million miles from the sun? Good. Then carry on, as you were."

We're full of it. We aren't mature. When I get home, I'm still going to pin my wife against the refrigerator, put my mouth on her neck and make raspberry sounds until she finds a way to smack me on the ears hard enough to get me to stop.

You can keep us from spending too much money on toys, but we will still want them and we'll still make an ironclad case as to why they are justified. Just don't fall for it.

So, if you are waiting for him to grow up, set your alarm for a million years from now and call me when it happens. I still won't believe it. But I'm fun to talk to.

ABOUT THE AUTHOR

Charles Herrick is a Seattle native. He married Kristy while in college and he feels that was the best decision of his life. They have three great kids, Lexie, Mason and Walker, along with llamas, two chickens and a bulldog named Bullard, who is very dull and dependent.

Charles is a writer and relief worker, serving alone in the most challenging settings in the underdeveloped world. He has been to the mud huts of Kenya, the slums of Bombay, and other places rarely mentioned in Condé Nast. In Africa he resolved an epidemic. In India he treated lepers and untouchables for all kinds of health ailment. Later in the high mountains of Southern India, he taught a woman to walk again who had been crippled since the age of 5 and who had not walked in 33 years.

With a Bachelor of Science degree in pre-medical studies and fresh out of the University of Washington, Charles "temporarily" entered the business world. There, with his hand perpetually on the doorknob, he spent the first couple of decades where he was highly successful, eventually becoming the CEO of one of Seattle's largest technology firms.

Of the 5000 people in Seattle who have worked for him at one time or another, approximately 80% love him; 15% could take him or leave him; and 5% will run him over in a crosswalk if they see him. This is an admirable distribution and one we should all strive for - especially if you look both ways before crossing the street.

He is the author of several books, including *Breath of Kenya*, which details the time he spent in a primitive village in the deep interior of East Africa.

To contact Charles, email him: charles@charlesherrick.com

www.ingramcontent.com/pod-product-compliance
Lightning Source LLC
Chambersburg PA
CBHW020431290526
45785CB00002B/796